PB EDU
J17-SS

Higher Education
into the 1990s

Higher Education into the 1990s

New Dimensions

To Commemorate the Jubilee of the
Society for Research into Higher Education
1964–1989

Edited by Sir Christopher Ball
and Heather Eggins

The Society for Research into Higher Education
and Open University Press

Published by SRHE and
Open University Press
12 Cofferidge Close
Stony Stratford
Milton Keynes MK11 1BY

and
1900 Frost Road, Suite 101,
Bristol, PA 19007, USA

First published 1989

British Library Cataloguing in Publication Data

Higher education into the 1990's: new dimensions.
  1. Great Britain. Higher education
  I. Ball, Christopher, *1935*–   II. Eggins, Heather
  III. Society for Research into Higher Education
  378.41

  ISBN 0-335-09223-3
  ISBN 0-335-09222-5 (paper)

Library of Congress Cataloging-in-Publication Data

Higher education into the 1990s: new dimensions / edited by Sir
  Christopher Ball, Heather Eggins.
      p.   cm.
    'To commemorate the jubilee of the Society for Research into
  Higher Education, 1964–1989.'
    Includes index.
    ISBN 0-335-09223-3.   ISBN 0-335-09222-5 (pbk.)
    1. Education, Higher – Aims and objectives.   2. Education, Higher–
  –Forecasting.   3. Society for Research into Higher Education.
  I. Ball, Christopher, 1935–   .   II. Eggins, Heather.   III. Society
  for Research into Higher Education.
  LB2325.H487   1989
  378'.009'049—dc20   89-8784 CIP

Typeset by Rowland Phototypesetting Limited
Bury St Edmunds, Suffolk
Printed in Great Britain by St Edmundsbury Press Limited
Bury St Edmunds, Suffolk

To Sir Hermann Bondi KCB FRS
President of the SRHE

Contents

The Contributors

Editors

Sir Christopher Ball, Kellogg Fellow, Oxford University Institute of External Studies, 1 Wellington Square, Oxford OX1 2JA.

Heather Eggins, Council for National Academic Awards, 344 Gray's Inn Road, London WC1X 8BP.

Contributors

Diana Green, Director of Academic Planning, City of Birmingham Polytechnic, Perry Barr, Birmingham B42 2SU.

Geoffrey Harding and Brian Kington, IBM United Kingdom Limited, South Bank, 76 Upper Ground, London SE1 9PZ.

Anthony O'Hear, Professor of Philosophy, University of Bradford, Richmond Road, Bradford BD7 1DP.

Victoria Phillips, 39 Birkbeck Mansions, Birkbeck Road, London N8 7PG.

Christopher Price, Director, Leeds Polytechnic, Calverley Street, Leeds LS1 3HE.

Naomi E. Sargant, Senior Commissioning Editor, Channel Four Television, 60 Charlotte Street, London W1P 2AX.

Peter Scott, Editor, *The Times Higher Education Supplement*, Priory House, St John's Lane, London EC1M 4BX.

Peter Slee, Head of Education Policy Group, Confederation of British Industry, Centre Point, 103 New Oxford Street, London WC1A 1DU.

Leslie Wagner, Director, The Polytechnic of North London, Holloway Road, London N7 8DB.

Professor Gareth Williams, Centre for Higher Education Studies, Institute of Education, University of London, 58/9 Gordon Square, London WC1H 0NT.

Kenneth Wilson, Principal, Westminster College, North Hinksey, Oxford OX2 9AT.

Acknowledgements

Chief among our acknowledgements must be Nicolas Malleson, the founder and first chairman of the Society for Research into Higher Education, whose jubilee this book is commemorating. It is a nice point that Nicolas Malleson's concern for the welfare of students within higher education (he was the Physician in charge of the University of London Health Service and Director of the Research Unit for student problems in the University of London) also led to an interest in the quality of higher education and the need for research into that subject. The Society has undergone shifts in emphasis since its founding in December 1964, but the relevance of the needs of students to its activities remains.

The thanks of the Editors also go to all the contributors to this volume who have willingly allowed themselves to be cajoled into meeting difficult deadlines so that the book can properly appear at the right date. We also wish to thank Dr Peter Knight, our current Chairman, for his support in this project, Rowland Eustace, SRHE's indefatigable administrator, whose extensive knowledge of the Society is invaluable, our secretaries for their help, and our families for their support. And finally we would each wish to extend our thanks to each other: working together has been a wholly enjoyable and pleasant experience, not least because the quality of the contributions has provided stimulating and interesting reading.

Introduction

Sir Christopher Ball

The pattern of events is difficult to discern. Historians compete to construct plausible accounts of the past. The present is too close to us to be seen clearly. The future is unknown, and largely unknowable. If mere description is difficult, explanation is even more so. And this is especially true in the realm of education in the United Kingdom, where there is no ready consensus about its purpose, nature and value. Where (some) other nations shape their educational systems to achieve national unity, wealth creation and personal fulfilment (in that order), here we argue whether the second or third of these desirable objectives should be given priority, and avert our gaze from the almost taboo subject of the need to create national unity in a multi-cultural society.

Higher education has not shown much interest in the vexed question of the aims of education. In spite of the Robbins Committee's valiant attempt to establish in 1963 four objectives for a properly balanced system of higher education,[1] for most of us it remains true that our first loyalty is to our discipline, to the single honours degree and to research. We find it difficult (and uncongenial) to raise our eyes from the particularities of disciplines (where advance is made by analysis and fragmentation) and attempt an overview and synthesis of the whole of higher education. Such a venture seems almost unscholarly.

And so it is – though not quite in the sense implied in the previous paragraph. The problem is that the observer is inside the experiment. All the contributors to this book, including the editors, must declare an interest and thereby claim what cannot properly be allowed – to be judges in their own cause. Higher education is the guardian of scholarly objectivity and scientific method: *quis custodiet ipsos custodes?* The constructive criticism of our system of higher education will remain difficult while those who are expert are not impartial, and those who are impartial are not thought to be expert.

Nevertheless, some things can be said. The fundamental challenge facing UK higher education since the middle of the twentieth century has been how to adapt an elite system to provide a popular model; when the history of higher education in the present century comes to be written, I believe that the painful transformation to a popular system will prove to be the key theme. The Robbins

Report, the development of the polytechnics, the conversion of the colleges of education, the work of the National Advisory Body and the government's White Paper of 1987[2] can be seen as successive attempts to increase access and promote educational opportunities for a wider range and larger proportion of members of our society. The social pressures leading to the continuous expansion of higher education are obvious, both in the United Kingdom and in other countries. Both student demand and employment needs have grown and, subject to demographic changes, are expected to continue to grow. The 1980 participation rate of 12.5 per cent had risen by 1988 to 15 per cent and is likely to exceed 20 per cent by 1995. Kenneth Baker, in a recent speech at the University of Lancaster, has contemplated a figure of 30 per cent as a long-term target.[3] The beginning of the twentieth century saw the marginalization of the universities of Oxford and Cambridge, when it became apparent that they could not provide the expansion then required. It now looks increasingly possible that the end of the century will see a similar marginalization of the 'traditional university system', leaving the task of expansion to the Open University, the polytechnics and the colleges of higher education.

In essence, the agenda for higher education is a simple one. For each generation the questions are the same, though the answers differ. How many students should be provided for? What and how should they learn? How best can we solve the cost-effectiveness equation? The Robbins Report assumed as an axiom that courses of higher education should be available for all those qualified by ability and attainment to pursue them who wished to do so. The present government has accepted the reformulation of that principle to the effect that the wish for higher education accompanied by the ability to benefit from it should determine access. If, as I believe, a serious aspiration for higher education is itself the critical determinant of ability to benefit, then we are close to answering the first question (How many students should be provided for?) as follows: courses of higher education should be available for all who seriously want them. In the absence (as yet) of effective marketing of courses to home students, it is difficult to guess at the scale of expansion needed to satisfy demand defined in that way. But I believe that Mr Baker's suggestion of a participation rate of 30 per cent will prove to be an underestimate.

What, and how, should they learn? This is an issue where oversimplification is both easy and fatal. I am not persuaded that we must choose between the extremes of 'learning for its own sake' and a narrowly instrumental theory of utilitarianism. I have some sympathy with the anonymous eighteenth-century writer who argued that 'duty's just study rightly reapplied'. In any event, informed student demand is probably a better guide than the wisdom of planners or the manpower forecasts of governments or employers. In future, good courses will have to satisfy three criteria: they must be *attractive* to prospective students, *rigorous* in the judgement of those responsible for teaching and *enabling*. Good courses enable students to achieve their objectives in life and work. The judgement of the 'enabling quality' of a course will be shared between teachers, students and employers.

The 'usefulness' debate is still in its infancy. But initiatives such as the Royal

Society of Arts (RSA) Capability Campaign or the Training Agency's scheme for 'Enterprise in Higher Education' show that the enabling value of courses will be one of the critical issues in the years to come. I welcome that. Students, employers and those responsible to the taxpayer for public funds have a right and a duty to pursue the issue.

The cost-effectiveness equation is a complex and controversial question. It involves consideration not only of the sources of funds (public or private) but also of the mechanisms for their distribution (funding agencies, fees, vouchers, etc.); not only the trade-off between quantity and quality of higher education but also the nature and definition of quality itself in this context. We must never forget that existing arrangements produce existing results. If we want something different (wider access, more enabling courses, for example), we must be prepared to change the system.

Higher education has been supported by a mixture of public and private funding ever since the state began to fund education. The question is not one of principle, but of balance between the two sources. In my view, whether we look for substantial expansion or merely the maintenance of the status quo, we must expect a partial shifting of the burden of funding higher education from the public purse to private resources. If this happens it will be important to ensure that the opportunities for the underprivileged members of society – who have never been well represented in higher education, in spite of a generous system of support for full-time students – are not further eroded.

It is too early to discern the funding strategies of the new funding bodies, the Polytechnics and Colleges Funding Council (PCFC) and the Universities Funding Council (UFC), but they will be of the highest importance. I hope they will encourage expansion. One of the most effective ways of doing this would be to shift the balance of funding from grant to fees. Full-time student fees (£607 in 1988–9) should be raised to two or three times that level, with corresponding decreases in UFC and PCFC grant, to encourage the marketing of courses and recruitment of new students.[4] If universities and polytechnics also decided to charge a supplementary fee (not recoverable from public funds) an effective channel for private funding of higher education would be created. Those who favour vouchers wish to go even further towards placing the responsibility for, and control of, the resourcing of higher education in the hands of student-clients.

For some years the concept of the unit of resource (the average funding available for the education of each student in the system, or parts of the system) has dominated the debate on the funding of higher education. There is a rough, but real, relationship between the level of resources and the quality of education. No one believes that a massive expansion of higher education is possible without a substantial increase of funding, whether from public or private sources (or both). But increases in efficiency are also possible. It is to be expected that the price of securing extra funding for the expansion of higher education will include the more efficient deployment of what is already available.

Quality is a slippery word. We use it somewhat indiscriminately to refer to the quality of the student's educational experience, to the quality of the student's ability and attainment (at entry to or exit from higher education), and to the 'value added' during the process of higher education. Those who say 'more means worse' are thereby selecting a particular quality measure – often the least important one, the A-level measure of ability and attainment at entry. If quality refers to added value or (as I prefer to think) fitness for purpose, then there is no reason why more should not mean better.

In brief, the challenge facing higher education during the 1990s will be whether it is prepared to change as it grows. More will mean different. An expanding system of higher education, offering enabling courses to a wider range of students, earning substantial private funding, and readily accountable both for the efficiency and quality of its activities, will also have every chance of securing substantially increased public funding. I see no other route out of the present impasse.

But, of course, such a programme of expansion and change will not be easy. Although it sometimes seems as if capacity is infinitely elastic, there must be a limit to the expansion that is possible without a major new capital building programme or the development of new institutions of higher education. The polytechnics and colleges, having expanded by more than 20 per cent during the 1980s, now have considerably less spare capacity than the universities – which have played little part in the recent growth of higher education. However, the non-university model is both cheaper and more readily accessible to the new students (mature, part-time, and without traditional qualifications) who must now be attracted. The role, and response, of the Open University is – and will be – critical. Should the Open University be truly open?

The role of research is also a problem. In an elite system of higher education it is possible to arrange for all teachers to be funded for a dual role, the education of students and the pursuit of fundamental research. In a popular system of higher education, that is neither possible nor sensible. While all who teach students in universities, polytechnics or colleges should pursue scholarship and advanced learning in order to stay at the forefront of their subject, fundamental research (which in science and technology is increasingly expensive) has to be concentrated in a limited range of exceptional departments and institutions. There is no logic in the assumption that the scale of fundamental research must be determined by the scale of higher education. Here, more probably does mean worse!

Concentration and selectivity in the funding of research will be one of the most awkward consequences of expansion, as the polytechnics have already found. I doubt whether by the end of the century the 45 existing universities will all be able to maintain the illusion that they are as much institutes of research as institutions of higher education. The Secretary of State's invitation to the UFC to separate the funding of teaching and research is the beginning of the end of the elite model of higher education.

Such a prospect seems to threaten the position and values of many of those who teach in higher education, particularly in the universities. And yet without their constructive co-operation, the agenda of expansion cannot be delivered. In the 'teaching-first' institutions of the future we shall need an imaginative and confident body of academic staff interested in concepts like continuing education, Credit Accumulation and Transfer, educational technology and distance learning. Outstanding leadership will be required to help staff take ownership of this new agenda. As in the schools, those who feel undervalued and underrewarded will find it difficult to offer a generous welcome to unfamiliar ideas and the challenge of expansion.

One aspect of that challenge is the recognition that higher education is not self-contained but part of the seamless web of life-long education. Expansion will not be aided by insistence on a clear distinction of level between further and higher education, or on the 'royal road' to university education through A level. We shall have to pay close attention to progression, not only making it possible for those who choose non-A-level routes at 16 to reach higher education (and benefit from it), but also developing a national awareness that (just as all roads lead to Rome) all educational routes offer opportunities for progression, and ensuring that there are indeed no dead ends. While we are about it we might reconsider the question of reforming A levels . . .

As the ideal of life-long learning begins to take root and to challenge the old idea of a sufficient initial education, the distinction between further and higher education will be hard to maintain. Already we are uneasily aware of the confusion between 'postgraduate in level' and 'postgraduate in time'. Much continuing education is postgraduate in time, but not in level.

The old certainties are fading. It is time to redefine the idea of 'higher' in higher education; to question whether concepts and terms like 'course' or 'institution' will continue to provide satisfactory analytical tools for its description; and, above all, to reconsider the purposes and customers of higher education. Although the future cannot be known in advance, one thing is certain – that it will be different. Change is inevitable.

The essays in this volume consider the development of higher education into the 1990s from many different points of view and in many contrasting dimensions. The tension between the past and the future, tradition and innovation, the elite and the popular model, the old order and new purposes, is readily apparent. We have sought contributors with a wide range of different experience, standpoints and convictions, from the Left and the Right, from teachers and students, from academics and industry, from both genders and either side of the binary line. Peter Scott's leading contribution on 'The Power of Ideas' opens with the sentence: 'Knowledge is at the heart of higher education.' We hope that this volume will contribute both to knowledge about, and (more importantly) to the understanding of, the present predicament and future potential of higher education. The book ends with Gareth Williams's essay on finance, which underlines the critical important of resources and their distribution. Individuals are sometimes moved by ideals; institutions never. Like all other institutions, universities, polytechnics and colleges are moved by their perceived interests. In education, as elsewhere, money talks.

Notes

1 These were: instruction in skills; the promotion of the general powers of the mind; the advancement of learning; and the transmission of a common culture and common standards of citizenship – see Committee on Higher Education, *Higher Education. Report of the Committee under the Chairmanship of Lord Robbins*, Cmnd 2154, HMSO, 1963. Compare also the joint statement of the UGC and NAB, *A Strategy for Higher Education in the Late 1980s and Beyond*, NAB, September 1984.
2 Department of Education and Science, *Higher Education: Meeting the Challenge*, Cm 114, HMSO, 1987.
3 See 'Baker's Vision for the Next 25 Years', *Times Higher Education Supplement*, 13 January 1989, p. 7.
4 The government seems to agree – see *Shifting the Balance of Public Funding of Higher Education to Fees: A Consultation Paper*, DES, April 1989.

1

The Power of Ideas

Peter Scott

Knowledge is at the heart of higher education. Its disciplines, academic and professional, are the categories that shape the pattern of teaching and research, the services which universities, polytechnics and colleges are organized to provide. In the context of modern higher education, of course, knowledge must be interpreted in the widest possible sense. It embraces not only the *what*, the content and methods of particular subjects, but also the *why*, the larger intellectual and cultural questions they provoke, and the *how*, their practical application to the solution of personal, social and economic problems. So knowledge, in this catholic sense, is not the exclusive property of a high intellectual civilization, and of those elite institutions most closely associated with the conservation, transmission and development of that civilization. It is not simply the business of the ivory towers. Knowledge, in this broad sense but on an increasingly sophisticated level, now permeates our mass society and industrial civilization. It is a – perhaps the – central commodity in the post-industrial society towards which Britain is rapidly evolving in the last decade of the twentieth century. It is not an accident that the term 'information society', to indicate a social configuration rather than simply a cluster of computer wires, has become popular.[1] Knowledge, of course, is as crucial a resource in the development of political democracy, the struggle for social justice and the progress towards individual enlightenment. It is no longer sacred and confined. So on any reasonable definition all higher education institutions, not just those universities angling for an 'R' classification,[2] are also knowledge institutions.

The purpose of this chapter is not to discuss in detail the nature of knowledge in modern higher education systems. Their expansion and elaboration have made this task more complex than ever before. Many of today's students neither come from nor are destined to join a cohesive elite; and many new subjects have been admitted to higher education, to supplement and perhaps dilute the old academic and professional canon. But to imagine that one consequence is a move away from knowledge may be a mistake. Despite the opening-out of higher education, knowledge, even in the restricted sense of sophisticated information and expert skills, remains at its heart. Those who seek to recast the aims of higher education in terms of process rather than product, of problem-solving rather than disciplinary content, have not always made out a convincing case.[3]

The purpose here is more limited – to reflect on the relationship between higher education as an intellectual system and as a political system, between its private and public lives, to borrow Martin Trow's useful terminology.[4] In the past this relationship has been difficult to characterize, at once intense and oblique. In a broad sense, higher education's private life has decisively shaped its public life. The expansion of the life sciences, in research output and student numbers, could not have taken place without the scientific revolution that in the 1950s began to transform biology and biochemistry (DNA and all that). But the nature of the link may be more complicated than it appears at first. The post-war growth of more elaborate health services and of the biomedical industry, which of course itself depended on these remarkable scientific break-throughs, also stimulated the development of life sciences in higher education in the 1960s and 1970s. So the causality, even the sequence, of this complicated relationship between intellectual origins and political outcomes is difficult to describe.

Of course, there are less ambiguous examples. There are many fields of engineering, with elaborate superstructures of courses and departments, con-sultancy and research, which depend utterly on the scientific breakthroughs that have led to new products and processes. Polymers are a straightforward case. On the other hand, the links between changes in the knowledge base of the human and social sciences (their private life), and in their position and prominence within higher education (their public life), are difficult to trace. For example, history as an academic discipline has been in inventive turmoil for more than a generation; old orthodoxies have been overthrown; new intellectual styles and priorities have been imported, often from across the Channel; and new cliometric techniques have been developed.[5] Yet, despite these qualitative changes, the position of history within universities and polytechnics has not been significantly modified. This academic excitement has largely been con-tained within changes in the curriculum of existing courses. It has been only modestly reflected in new kinds of courses, for example part-time Master of Arts degrees in family or local history. So the relationship between intellectual and political change seems, at best, diffuse.

In terms of public policy, that relationship has been even more difficult to establish. Where it has existed at all, ideas have depended on institutions rather than the other way round. New forms of professional training, for which there has been a clear political utility, have had grafted onto them an intellectual superstructure.[6] Much of the growth of the social sciences in the post-war university can perhaps be attributed to the rapid development of the welfare state as much as to the intellectual vitality of core disciplines like sociology and psychology. A similar phenomenon can be observed in relation to business studies and management. The political success of the latter subjects probably owes little to subtler insights into economics or organizational theory. Conversely, the declining esteem in which the more theoretical social sciences are now held is not the result of any loss of academic creativity.

In general, however, links between higher education's private and public lives have become difficult to describe. Two broad explanations are plausible. The first is that in the mid-twentieth century the academy enjoyed exceptional prestige. The old power of the dons within a university system intimately related to the nation's elite was reinforced by the new power of the code-breakers, atom scientists and social engineers of the post-war great and good. No longer dependent on student fees or on civic and industrial support but subsidized, at arm's length, by the state, universities, and to a lesser extent other higher education institutions, were more autonomous than ever before (or since?). Because of their own prestige as a profession and the heightened autonomy of the institutions in which they worked, scientists and scholars achieved an unprecedented command over the intellectual agenda.[7] In any case that agenda rested on a firm liberal consensus in which all elite groups, political as well as academic, concurred. So there was little basis on which to interfere with higher education's private life, and little desire to do so.

The second explanation is that the 30 years from 1950 to 1980 were a period of rapid growth in higher education. The number of students more than trebled and 20 universities and 30 polytechnics were established (at a rate of more than one a year!). As a result of this exceptional growth, the clash of priorities within higher education was blunted. Because most reasonable demands could be satisfied there was no need for outside intervention to adjudicate between the respective claims of, say, English and physics. The public life of higher education was preoccupied by the rational management of headlong growth, by issues of quantity rather than of quality. There was no motive to question the intellectual agenda established by particular disciplines. So the private life of higher education was left alone.

This does not mean that the intellectual agenda remained undisturbed. Dramatic as the changes in higher education's public life have been, they are much less spectacular than the endless revolutions in its private life. Universities today still have much in common with universities a generation ago. Even polytechnics bear some marks of their origins in technical education, teacher training and the world of art and design. Institutions cannot be transformed overnight. They are carriers of deeply entrenched values and routines that are difficult to overturn. But disciplines change at a bewildering speed. Physics in the 1980s is not really the same subject as physics in the 1950s. Even arts subjects like English literature and philosophy are utterly changed. To borrow another metaphor that illuminates this contrast between the intellectual and political aspects of higher education, the invisible college is many times more radical than the visible college. Or, to be more exact, its conservatism is of a different quality. It is a conservatism of tradition not status, of values not structures. Disciplines have loyalties and routines as fierce as those of institutions. But they are not the same.

Neither of these conditions any longer applies. The academy no longer enjoys great prestige on which higher education can build a successful claim to political autonomy. The mid-century consensus has collapsed. At the same time the exceptional post-war growth of higher education has come to an end, in terms of resources if not of students.[8] Each of these changes has made it more difficult to maintain the old loose relationship between the political and intellectual aspects of higher education, or the informal concordat between its public and private lives. Because of the declining prestige of the academy, the autonomy of the universities has been eroded and polytechnics and colleges, despite their academic maturity, have been firmly discouraged from pursuing autonomist ambitions. Institutions are no longer permitted to devise their own priorities, priorities intimately related to the private world of disciplines, but must instead respond more exactly to national needs that are defined outside the academy. The collapse of the mid-century consensus, which in the broadest sense was liberal, has provoked an outbreak of ideological warfare on a scale not experienced in Britain since the earlier years of the reign of Queen Victoria. As a result the intellectual agenda is fiercely fought over. Finally, the end of growth has forced the managers of higher education institutions, guided by their political paymasters and advised by an expanding corps of policy-makers, to adjudicate between the claims of particular disciplines far more frequently and decisively than in the past. Because of the need to establish clearer and harsher priorities, there has been a strong swing away from collegial and towards managerial government in higher education.[9] Public order has had to be imposed on its anarchic private world.

As a result these two worlds, the public and private, have begun to grind up against each other during the 1980s – and there is every sign that the friction between these political and intellectual spheres will become even greater during the remaining years of the century. Once movements in higher education policy were confined almost exclusively to the system's public life; its private life was left in the safe custody of the academic, or professional, great and good. The supreme example of this arrangement, of course, was the University Grants Committee (UGC). Within the UGC subjects always came first and institutions second. It was only when the subject committees had had their say that the implications for institutions of their proposals were considered.

In the last five years that relationship has been reversed. Institutions now command disciplines. In 1986 the UGC ranked all university departments according to the quality of their research on a four-point scale ranging from 'outstanding' to 'below average'. Although the detailed work of discrimination was left to subject committees (supplemented in some cases by *ad hoc* inquiries), the initiative itself came from the main committee which, bowing to political and economic pressures, had decided to allocate funds to universities more selectively. This exercise provoked great controversy, particularly in less favourably ranked departments. It was objected to partly because of its acknowledged political purpose and partly on technical grounds, but also because it was seen as an invasion of the private life of universities, a gross intrusion by politicians from outside higher education and managers within into academic questions that could only be answered by subject specialists. There were even those who argued that such comparative assessments were themselves improper, even if undertaken by established experts and for the most innocent of political purposes.

Such feelings have not been confined to the universities, although they have been most intense there. The Council for National Academic Awards (CNAA), which is responsible for validating or accrediting degrees in polytechnics and colleges, has also been reluctant to offer comparative judgements about the quality of courses and departments. When the former National Advisory Body (NAB) embarked on the rationalization of town planning, the most that the CNAA would agree to do was to identify those courses of exceptional quality. Even this limited exercise in discrimination was bitterly opposed. The CNAA may find it as difficult to collaborate with the Polytechnics and Colleges Funding Council (PCFC), especially as the former now has less detailed academic information about institutions following the move to loose-rein accreditation. Its reticence is reinforced, of course, by the character of its evolving relationship with institutions. That relationship is still more academic than political. It depends for its effectiveness on mutual trust. Information acquired for validating courses, or accrediting institutions, still has to be regarded as largely privileged. The CNAA, therefore, is part of higher education's private life, despite its political superstructure. The failure to understand this was at the root of many of the confused criticisms of the CNAA during the 1980s (although cruder political motives were also important) – for example, that it was ineffective because it failed to take action in cases such as that of the sociology and applied social studies degrees at the Polytechnic of North London;[10] and that its bureaucracy stifled the initiative of institutions.[11] But there is little hope that such misunderstandings will be cleared up in the 1990s. The prospect is the reverse, that those agencies that form part of higher education's private life will be further politicized. The UGC has already gone; the CNAA has only just survived. Public bodies that embody private values will come to be regarded as anachronisms.

Another example of the friction between the political and intellectual spheres of higher education is the controversy provoked by attempts to make greater use of performance indicators in planning the system, not just its managerial structure but also its academic character.[12] Because teaching and research are at the heart of the enterprise many of the suggested indicators concern matters once regarded as the private business of subject specialists. To measure how institutions manage their cash flows is generally accepted to be a legitimate exercise. Even the need to compare staff–student ratios is acknowledged. But attempts to develop quantitative measures of academic performance are regarded with great suspicion, and even contempt. The assessment of quality is seen as a matter for judgement by peers rather than measurement by managers.

Yet, despite these doubts, performance indicators have acquired growing importance. The Economic and Social Research Council has attempted to improve PhD performance by measuring the rate at which research students complete their doctorates, and by penalizing those institutions and departments with poor completion rates. The various subject reviews undertaken by the UGC also relied heavily on quantitative measures, for example to determine the minimum size for economically and scientifically viable departments.[13] Planning agencies, in their evaluation of institutions, and institutions themselves, in their evaluation of faculties, departments and individual staff members, have made increasing use of bibliometric techniques and league tables of research and other income.

One reason for this sustained invasion of higher education's private life, if that is not too strong a description, is that peer review, the traditional means by which academic quality is measured, is widely seen as too feeble an instrument to manage institutions under new and urgent pressures, political and economic. Peer review is essentially a conservative mechanism; its purpose is to maintain academic quality. It cannot help managers to make comparative judgements between disciplines; nor is it well designed to measure differences in academic performance. Another less significant reason is that, like all advanced nations, the United Kingdom has become a data-driven society. The age of the incisive minute and the elegant report is over. The age of computer-compatible management information has arrived. The qualitative must be reduced, or transposed, to the quantitative before it can become relevant to the making of public policy. But the main reason is the shifting of the boundary between higher education's public and private lives. This shift reflects a profoundly changed view of the role of higher education and of the function of knowledge that has come to be accepted in these last years of the twentieth century. The academy is no longer seen as a semi-independent estate of the nation with crucial fiduciary responsibilities; and knowledge is defined more and more in terms of utilitarian outcomes rather than of liberal intentions, of externalities rather than the development of human understanding.

There is little prospect of this shift being reversed and of higher education's private world being depoliticized. It is not even clear that this would be desirable. The cultural and economic conditions that sustained the system's academic privacy no longer apply. In a mass higher education system, which Britain's universities, polytechnics and colleges are rapidly becoming, the autonomy of the disciplines is more difficult to justify. It degenerates too easily into a backward-looking inwardness which not only inhibits wider access but suppresses academic enterprise. After all, disciplines are micro-political systems in their own subtle ways. They are not, and never were, little Edens, to be contrasted with the cruel politico-managerial wilderness into which higher education has now been cast! In any case, there can be no return to an older configuration of the system in which autonomous academic values enjoyed a natural precedence over social, economic and political demands.

So in the 1990s higher education has a threefold task – to tackle the difficult technical problems that arise from attempts to measure academic performance both effectively and accurately; to develop national and institutional policies that reward successful management without abridging academic freedom; and to ensure that efforts to make both teaching and research more appropriate to the actual circumstances of late twentieth-century UK society do not inhibit their capacity to transcend the 'givenness' of our present condition. In short, a new balance must be struck between higher education as a political system and as an intellectual system.

The first of these tasks is the most immediate. There is already an urgent need to improve the way in which academic quality is assessed and academic performance measured, and in particular how these assessments and measurements are related. The experience of the UGC suggests that there is still a lot to learn. Its first attempt to evaluate the research performance of university departments was widely criticized, as has already been noted. The UGC was accused of relying on incomplete or inappropriate data and confidential advice. Yet when the UGC came in 1988 to attempt a second evaluation, its approach was substantially unchanged. On the other side of the binary line, the new PCFC is in no better position than the NAB was in the mid-1980s to relate agreed quality assessments to the funding of polytechnics and colleges. It, like the NAB, has to rely on an unsatisfactory mishmash of advice and intelligence from Her Majesty's Inspectors, validating agencies and professional bodies.

There are three reasons for this distressing lack of progress. The first is simply the lack of accurate and effective techniques. Present procedures for counting the number of publications by members of staff or the amount of extra income earned by departments are either banal or ridiculous. In some cases, they add little to the information already available; in others, their crude and spurious methods may give misleading impressions of actual academic worth.

The second is that, even when accurate and acceptable measures have been devised, they are often difficult to interpret. Are high completion rates evidence of effective teaching or of a lack of rigour? Without independent (and intimate?) knowledge of the institutions being compared it may be difficult to say. Performance indicators ask as many questions as they answer.[14] There is a particular difficulty when different measures have to be combined to produce an overall assessment of an individual's, department's or institution's performance. How are the weights attached to different measures to be decided?

The third reason is that far too little is known about the inner life of disciplines. With a few honourable exceptions intellectual history has been a neglected field.[15] Also it has tended to concentrate on large-scale questions related to the intellectual culture of nations and epochs, rather than on the micro-cultures of particular disciplines. Nor has this neglect been made good by sociologists. The development of the academic profession(s) has received little attention – again with honourable exceptions.[16] But without knowledge of the founding, and enduring, intentions of disciplines it is difficult to measure academic outcomes convincingly. It is a little like planning a military campaign without maps.

This does not mean that the campaign will, or should, be called off. Managerial decisions and academic judgements will inevitably be increasingly entwined in the 1990s.Crucial questions, like the need for a super-league of research universities, the critical mass for viable departments in a range of subjects, the relationship between teaching and research and non-standard entry to encourage wider access, are both academic and political. What it does mean is that managers responsible for planning the system must provide themselves with adequate maps. The only feasible way to acquire decent academic intelligence is some combination of peer review and performance measures. The particular mix between the two, of course, will have to vary from subject to subject, by level and type of course, perhaps also by sector and institution. And, if this academic intelligence is to be effectively but fairly applied, there must be open and firm rules to govern its collection and use. For example, information collected for one purpose should not be used for another without the most careful consideration and clearest possible consultation – not because this might be unfair, but because it might be misleading.

The second task is almost as immediate. It is to plan higher education to meet national needs (or, if ministers prefer, to make it accountable to its customers through some contrived market) without compromising those freedoms that are at the root of good teaching and research. After all, the state cannot plan for, nor the market demand, academic creativity, although the former can establish the conditions in which such creativity flourishes and the latter can help order its priorities. Higher education is first an intellectual system, and only second a political one. Its public life is contingent on its private life. This is not because of the superior claims of autonomous thought, of free intellectual inquiry, although in a liberal democracy these are formidable claims, but because knowledge, in the broad sense of the *what*, the *why* and the *how*, is the whole point of higher education. If the conditions that encourage the formation of knowledge are removed, the system loses its political utility. So the autonomy of the disciplines is not a privilege but a duty. This point requires particular emphasis at the start of a decade in which higher education policy seems likely to be dominated far too much by ideas of sales, in the shape of sophisticated public relations and marketing, and of management, in the form of elaborate information and control systems. Knowledge, whether it leads to culture or to skills, is higher education's only good. The rest is process.

The practical implications of such a view are difficult to catalogue. Perhaps the most important is that central to the planning of higher education should be the notion of academic productivity, perhaps even fecundity. This term, of course, must embrace far more than the efficient management of highly educated and skilled staff, expensive facilities for research and costly plant and buildings. It must also embrace more than effective and appropriate teaching and impressive lists of publications. It must seek to go wider, to assess the total intellectual enterprise of a department, faculty, institution, sector or even system. The keynote of such assessment should be eclecticism rather than reductionism. The aim should be an academic audit that is both sensitive and comprehensive rather than an aggregation of performance measures. So management styles and systems that have the effect of narrowing choices, limiting participation and simplifying inputs are likely to be inappropriate. Attempts to limit the powers of, rather than reform, academic boards and senates may lead to an intellectual diseconomy far more serious than the political shortcomings they are designed to confront. Getting the balance right between academic effectiveness and political efficiency is perhaps the most difficult task facing higher education in the 1990s.

But the most important, in the 1990s as in every decade, is the third task. This is to ensure that efforts to make teaching more effective in, and research more relevant to, the actual circumstances the United Kingdom will face in the 1990s do not inhibit higher education's responsibility to transcend the 'givenness' of our contemporary condition. There should be no conflict here, for the modern world, too, depends for its vitality on this capacity to see, and go, beyond the frontiers of present possibilities. Indeed this is almost a precondition of modernity, in science and in culture. But, of course, there will be conflict. This is most apparent in the awkward taxonomy of pure, strategic and applied research. As a result resources have drifted away from curiosity-driven research. Any funding system that uses the ability to attract research income from industry as an indication of successful performance and reinforces it with matching funds discriminates against frontier research where such support is by definition unavailable. It shrinks scientists' horizons by encouraging them to concentrate on today's manageable problems rather than on tomorrow's intractable ones.

There is a risk that during the 1990s the same shortening of perspectives, which is the inevitable product of increased emphasis on relevance and accountability because both can only be judged in the short term, will spread to affect the whole of higher education. The balance of postgraduate courses has already been tilted towards the practical, partly by the deliberate policies of the Department of Education and Science, research councils and other agencies, and partly because the sclerosis of the academic profession has undermined the attractions of PhDs and other more academic courses. A similar bias in favour of the vocational can also be observed in undergraduate education, although with less clear-cut results. Among students accountancy has flourished but most forms of engineering have languished (no doubt because of the chronic lack of good science and mathematics teachers in schools). Demand for the humanities has remained strong, reflecting the growing proportion of female students and the lesser obstacle they seem to present to mature and other non-standard entrants. The pattern of undergraduate education is made up of a chaotic accumulation of very personal choices in which aptitude, prejudice, temperament and ambition are confused. It is far more difficult to manage from above than are postgraduate courses and research. But the conformist pressures will also come from below. The imposition of a national curriculum in schools will tend to reduce the breadth, and certainly the heterodoxy, of undergraduate education. So the danger of a slide towards short-termism, and a shrinking of intellectual horizons, exists here, too.

That is one prospect for the 1990s – shrunken horizons in higher education's private life that ominously outweigh the new dimensions in its public life. It would make more difficult 'the social reconstruction of reality, the reordering of things-as-they-are so they are no longer experienced as given but rather as willed, in accordance with convictions about how things ought to be'.[17] Robert Darnton, the American historian, is writing here of the French Revolution but the same idea can be applied much more widely to the whole of modern science and culture – which perhaps is appropriate in the light of that revolution's crucial role in shaping the intellectual geography of the modern world. But there is a second, more hopeful, prospect. Far from constraining higher education's private life, the more intimate engagement of the system's political and academic values may give rise to a fuller mutual understanding – an academic world more alert to its social and political context, and a political world more sensitive to reason and more civilized in its search for truth. In this new age both donnishness and philistinism would fade away. It could no longer be said that the United Kingdom enjoyed a brilliant academic civilization but possessed an impoverished intellectual culture. Ideas as well as institutions would then become outward-bound. Which of these two very different prospects is more likely to take hold in the 1990s cannot be resolved, or even adequately debated, within a short chapter. The question can only be broached – but with the conviction that there is no other more important for higher education, in both its public and private lives, and the nation.

Notes

1 Daniel Bell, *The Coming of the Post-industrial Society*, Basic Books, 1973.
2 Advisory Board for the Research Councils, *A Strategy for the Science Base*, HMSO, 1987.
3 See William Birch, *The Challenge to Higher Education*, Open University Press, 1988.
4 Martin Trow, *Problems in the Transition from Elite to Mass Higher Education*, Centre for Studies in Higher Education Policy, University of California, 1973.
5 See Lawrence Stone, *The Past and the Present*, Routledge and Kegan Paul, 1981.
6 Robert Dingwall and Philip Lewis (eds), *The Sociology of the Professions*, Macmillan, 1984.
7 Margaret Archer, *Social Origins of Educational Systems*, London, 1979.
8 Department of Education and Science, *Higher Education: Meeting the Challenge*, Cm 114, HMSO, 1987.
9 Committee of Vice Chancellors and Principals, *Report of the Steering Group on University Efficiency* (Jarratt Report), Committee of Vice Chancellors and Principals, 1985.
10 Department of Education and Science, *Report of HM Inspectors on the Polytechnic of North London: BSc Sociology and BA Applied Social Studies Courses*, HMSO, 1983.
11 Department of Education and Science, *Academic Validation in Public Sector Higher Education* (Lindop Report), Cmnd 9501, HMSO, 1985.
12 Committee of Vice Chancellors and Principals/University Grants Committee, *University Management Statistics and Performance Indicators*, CVCP, 1987, and CVCP/UGC, *University Management Statistics and Performance Indicators in the UK*, CVCP, 1988.
13 University Grants Committee, *The Future of University Physics* HMSO, 1988, and UGC, *University Chemistry – The Way Forward*, HMSO, 1988.
14 Martin Cave, Steven Hanney, Maurice Kogan and Gillian Trevett, *The Use of Performance Indicators in Higher Education: a Critical Analysis of Developing Practice*, Jessica Kingsley, 1988.
15 Stefan Collini, Donald Winch and John Burrow, *That Noble Science of Politics: A Study in Nineteenth-century Intellectual History*, Cambridge University Press, 1984.
16 A. H. Halsey and Martin Trow, *The British Academics*, Faber and Faber, 1971.
17 Robert Darnton, 'What was Revolutionary about the French Revolution?', *New York Review of Books*, 19 January 1989.

2

The University as a Civilizing Force

Anthony O'Hear

From the observations I will be making in this paper it will be obvious that I am not in sympathy with many of the 'new dimensions' of education, higher or otherwise, referred to in the title of the present volume. I hope that in our rush to greet the next decade or the next century or to enter the next dimension we do not forget what we have learned from the old and unthinkingly destroy the inheritance with which we have been blessed and which we have done nothing to deserve.

In my title I have chosen to speak of the university, rather than of higher education. This is quite deliberate. I believe that there is an essential civilizing function which can be fulfilled only by what I am calling the 'university'. It will become apparent that not all 'universities' are universities in this sense, and perhaps that some institutions which are not called universities are 'universities' in my sense. The debasement of the linguistic coin is nowhere more apparent than in the field of education. What is important, though, is that we do not allow the *faux-monnayeurs* of educational policy to obscure from our view a certain form of higher education, which, since Newman, has been associated with the name university. It is indeed Newman's vision I am about to adumbrate. When I have done that, I shall briefly consider two objections to Newman, one fairly easily pushed aside, but the other rather more worrying because it reflects a deep pessimism about the intellectual and moral fibre of our time.

The idea of a university

People coming to Newman for the first time are often struck by the distinction he makes in the Preface to *The Idea of a University*[1] between universities and research institutes and academies, but this distinction is actually central to his thinking. He writes that there are 'other institutions far more suited to act as instruments of . . . extending the boundaries of our knowledge than a university'. In these other institutions, the teaching of undergraduates need be no part of the enterprise, and may actually interfere with it. In a university, by contrast, the teaching of undergraduates will be central. For, as we shall see, the task of the university will be to turn out an elite of people who are educated in a broad sense, who are not just specialists, but who have been enabled by their time at a university to see how their specialism may be brought into what F. R. Leavis referred to as 'effective relation with informed general intelligence, human culture, social conscience and political will'.[2] In other words, universities should aim at producing a type of person educated in a particular type of way, who through his education is disposed to see and look at things in a particular way, in the light perhaps of the best that has been thought and known, but certainly with the intellectual virtues of rationality, humility and patience. And pushing back the frontiers of knowledge is not directly relevant to this task. But there is, I believe, a deeper reason for distinguishing the aim of research from that of the liberal university: in the humanities, which, as we will see, must be the heart of the university, the very idea of extending the boundaries of knowledge is open to question.

The idea of knowledge having a boundary or frontier is entirely natural when one thinks of scientific knowledge. The growth of scientific knowledge is a matter of discovering more about the natural world, and this can be seen in terms of the discovery of new entities and new regularities and in terms of the postulation of new and deeper accounts of the fundamental processes governing natural phenomena. We can think of both the discovery of new entities and regularities and the postulation of more fundamental explanations of natural phenomena in terms of pushing back the frontiers of knowledge, for in both types of case we are discovering hitherto unknown aspects of a natural world which has an existence and reality separate from and independent of our knowledge. Here we have a firm grip on the notion of extending the frontiers of knowledge.

When we come to consider the humanities, however, this notion becomes far more problematic, even in an area like history, where there are certainly facts to be learned and discovered. But at least part of history, and in some ways the most important part, is how we are to regard our past and how we are to look at the forces that have made us what we are, and hence at what we are and what we might become. Take, for example, the range of questions raised by what might be called the historicist view of history, the view that there is a logic to history and an inevitable march of history in a certain direction. It is not at all clear that there are any particular historical facts, or any groups of such facts which could make us decide on the truth or falsity of this vision, though the vision will undoubtedly guide us in the selection and marshalling of our historical evidence. The progressivist-historicist model is undoubtedly extremely deeply rooted in our consciousness and in our ways of thinking, so much so that its grip is extremely hard to loosen, and it becomes hard to accept that – to take an example from the history of music – Sibelius and Richard Strauss are just as significant figures in twentieth-century music as, say, Schoenberg and Stravinsky. To write a non-progressive account of music, as of anything else, depends not so much on one's grasp of the historical facts, such as they may be, as on a particular sensitivity and disposition in the face of the facts, and in face of the progressivist rhetoric of our time.

I do not know whether one should say that the progressivist version of the history of a particular facet of experience is false and the opposing version correct, or vice versa. In the absence of an observer-independent set of data which the question may be said to be about, I am not sure that it is even right to put the question in terms of right and wrong, truth and falsity. Unlike the investigation of the natural world, what is at issue here is not so much the facts as our attitude to them, and, in the end, our attitude to ourselves. It is not the facts which determine the validity or otherwise of historicist histories, nor are historicist histories explanatory in the way that a formula such as Newton's second law explains the movements of the planets by predicting and quantifying their positions. In so far as Newton's account is correct, it shows us how the planets could not behave other than they do, because it shows us the principles on which they are operating. To talk about the breakdown of classical tonality and the movement towards atonality and serialism, by contrast, explains nothing that had to happen. At most it gives us the concepts and reasons under which Schoenberg and his followers conceived and justified their work in the period following 1910, but there was nothing inevitable about this, nothing which had to be or indeed which has to be, as indeed, despite the propaganda of the progressivists, the example of musicians who did not take Schoenberg's path shows.

The reason why history as a discipline has a central place in the humanities is because historical understanding is not primarily a case of unearthing an observer-independent reality. From the point of view of the present, the reality history deals with is certainly independent of us, but in dealing with it we are not trying to discover timeless laws governing human behaviour so much as to tell a story relevant to the way we conceive ourselves. Thus giving a historicist or anti-historicist interpretation of events of the past will have a close relationship to how we think of what we are and how we should act in our own time. And the same goes for other approaches to the past: for one's attitude to political history or economic history, for a Gibbonian interpretation of the Roman empire, or for a Burkean attitude to the French Revolution. I am not saying that the evidence does not on occasion favour one or other of these versions of the past, or cannot be made to favour it by a skilful historian, but that the ultimate acceptability and acceptance of one or other of these versions will both be influenced by and have a bearing on one's self-image and one's understanding of one's own time. And what goes for history will also go for the other humanities: for the attitudes one takes to particular works of art and literature, and to theses in philosophy.

I see the humanities as central to any university education, because the group one hopes to see emerging from the university will, above all, be a group concerned with and in some sense adept at the Leavisite task of bringing specialist knowledge and training into effective relationship with informed general intelligence, humane culture, social conscience and political will. It is in and through the humanities that we reflectively explore this relationship, because it is in the humanities that we attend most directly to questions concerning not only what we are, but also what we might become. Of course, the natural sciences have an essential role here: both what we are and what we might become are circumscribed by the natural world, and by our relationship as human beings to the natural world. Part, and a very important part, of our conception of self must be supplied by our knowledge of the natural world. The natural sciences, then, will form an essential ingredient in the discovery of self and human possibility, and will, therefore, be an essential component of any university. A university is not simply a liberal arts college, for a liberal arts college will lack half of what is needed for the production of *informed* general intelligence. But it is not in and through the natural sciences that we come to terms, humanly speaking, with whatever it is we learn in science about the natural world and our place in it. That question is addressed in the humanities, in philosophy, in history and in art and literature, and it is for that reason that I see the humanities as central to the specific function of the university.

In Newman's *Idea of a University*, the rationale for grouping students and teachers from diverse disciplines together in one institution is seen as being the production in individuals of that 'true enlargement of mind which is the power of viewing many things at once as one whole, of referring them severally to their true place in the universal system, of understanding their respective values, and determining their mutual dependence'.[3] A liberally educated man – the ideal product of the university – will possess knowledge 'not only of things, but of their mutual and true relations': he will see the particular discipline in which he specializes in terms of its place in the whole of knowledge, and in the way in which it contributes to and is suffused by that whole.

Newman is very far from opposing a deep knowledge of one particular discipline. Indeed, he believes firmly that 'a smattering in a dozen branches of study' is shallowness, a dissipation of mind rather than progress or true education. A rigorous immersion in one particular branch of study is a real education of the mind. It is only through engaging with a form of knowledge at an advanced level that one comes to understand what it is to submit oneself to the demands of reasoned enquiry. For this reason alone, there should be institutions in which people are taught at the highest level. But what is wanted over and above that – which may remain at the level of mere learning, useful to others maybe, but not to its possessor – is the wisdom that comes from the possession of a connected view and grasp of things. Newman distinguishes this cast of mind from what he calls 'viewiness', that tendency to the instant production of an opinion on any subject whatever, which is the province of journalism and the mass media and which journalism and the mass media foster. The critical methods and stringent demands of university disciplines ought to enable one to resist temptations to this sort of viewiness. It is Newman's hope that contact with teachers of one's own discipline who have sympathy and communion with scholars from other disciplines, together with contact with students from other disciplines, all of whom are working at their subjects at a level appropriate to a full and adequate understanding of their disciplines, will help to produce in the minds of those studying in universities 'the clear, calm and accurate vision and comprehension of all things, as far as the finite mind can embrace them, each in its place, and with its own characteristics upon it'.[4]

It is no doubt unfashionable to see the aim of any sort of education as the cultivation in the minds of the uninitiated of a sort of wisdom, as opposed to skills, techniques, information or money-earning capacities. But Newman is unashamedly platonic about education, seeing its end in the improvement of individual minds. He would entirely have accepted the point of Socrates's warning in the *Phaedrus*[5] about the invention of writing on the grounds that the written word can be anti-educational. Writing will lead men to rely on external marks rather than on knowledge they have properly assimilated and taken into their hearts. Such men, the precursors of today's information technologists, will know nothing themselves and have the conceit of wisdom, rather than wisdom itself. According to Socrates these conceited empty-heads will be a burden to their fellows; certainly they will have repudiated any sense of the true point or worth of knowledge, as contributing to one's wholeness and sensitivity as a human being. And Newman's vision of the university is that it should be an institution fostering the development of individuals of a certain type. This, to repeat, is the rationale for having different disciplines and scholars, teachers and students all grouped together under one roof.

According to Newman, the way a university might help to produce the philosophic cast of mind he seeks will largely be through the tradition and atmosphere of a place in which the cultivation of the intellect is valued for its own sake. In such a place, there will be teachers versed in the various disciplines who are, at the same time, in some sort of collaborative contact with those in other disciplines, and students from different places and backgrounds. Such an institution will define its own interrelationships, establish its own rules, and gain its own tone and character.

The ivory tower

I know from experience that many are shocked by the very idea of a university, as conceived by Newman and Leavis. They are shocked by the way an institution such as this will in effect be claiming for itself a privileged status, unaccountable in any direct way to the society in which it exists, and which will, as things stand at the moment, be paying for it. And, even worse, from the point of view of the democratic populism which often informs this type of criticism, the university will not only determine its own development and growth, it will also determine whom it will allow to come under its shadow. Universities are, in other words, unaccountable and elitist, and this is unacceptable in the 1990s.

It is worth pointing out that in objecting to the university as an ivory tower the political Left and Right are united. Both would prefer to see institutions of higher education renouncing any autonomous or privileged status, opening their doors to all-comers, involving themselves with 'real' issues and needs and subject to market forces or political imperative. Both would say that in my concentration on the cultural and educational role of universities, I have neglected their duty to serve the science-based, technological and democratic society whose funding makes their very existence possible. Universities now must concentrate on turning out trained engineers, managers, businessmen, social workers and the like, just as in the past they produced people suited for vocations, such as the law, the church and medicine.

It will also be said that the liberally educated man is one well able to contribute to society in various ways. But while this is true, to make that the end of the exercise will be to help destroy it, for the liberally educated mind is produced by the practice of disinterested study and reflection. Equally, without denying some scope in a university for service functions, it must be emphasized that a university cannot subordinate its educational function to its service role and continue to do that for which it is particularly suited and which, as Newman saw, provides the reason for grouping all the major intellectual disciplines in one institution.

Universities also have, necessarily and unfashionably, to be elitist institutions, transmitting at the highest level and contributing to the development of the best that has been thought and known, those traditions of thought and experience which can contribute most to our potential for knowledge, expressiveness and self-understanding. Not only is work at the highest level essential to the acquisition of the wisdom one is looking for in university graduates. The traditions themselves will die unless they are passed on to the next generation at a serious level, and a culture is civilized to the extent that it values its literary, artistic and scientific traditions. It is just implausible to suppose that more than a minority, possibly a small minority, are really capable of entering into the best that has been thought and known at the highest level. On the other hand, a civilized society will be one which values within itself the presence of such a group, a group whose quality of mind will affect and improve the quality of life in everyone else in that society through its influence and teaching, and through nurturing those traditions on which its claim to be civilized largely rests.

I have been publicly attacked (by a contributor to this volume) for daring to utter this view, on the grounds that my position is an assault on democracy. It is certainly an assault on egalitarianism. Whether it is an assault on democracy is not so clear. In the first place, to repeat – for whatever reason (I do not go into that) – as things are, not a great number of people will ever be able to really get to grips with Aeschylus or Plato or Plutarch or Milton or Kant or Eliot or the theory of evolution or Newtonian physics or quantum theory. Yet, surely for cultural continuity and health, we need some who can, who can lead and teach the rest of us in this respect. Again, I see it as pre-eminently the work of the university to provide us with such people, who are specialists in what they know, but not narrowly so, but who are sensitive to the human significance of what they know. I emphasize teaching here; one of the hoped-for advantages of the new licensed teacher scheme is to get more first-rate university people into teaching.

So my view is elitist and anti-egalitarian, although I see the elite I am interested in in terms of the genial influence it should have on the rest of society, through its influence and teaching, rather than as a closed and exclusive caste. Is this un- or anti-democratic? Well, I do not say the academic elite should rule, and perhaps they will be in an important sense, as Nietzsche thought, unfitted to ruling. But I would worry about a democracy, such as the one Dewey envisaged, in which the worth of an opinion or a tradition was to be measured by the extent to which it can be communicated to all and sundry. If our democracy is like that, then I am undemocratic, because I see a value in our literary, artistic, historical and scientific traditions, which is quite independent of their universal communicability. As far as the actual world goes, it may be forever beyond the reach of the mass of the population. In some ways the uncommunicable part will be the most important part, for it will be that part in which alertness and sensitivity and knowledge are at their maximum. But there need be nothing sinister in this. I will never be able to converse on equal terms about his subject to a mathematical physicist, but I can perfectly easily see that it is a good thing for his study to exist. The aim of people in university education should not be to track down to the lowest level, but, through their influence and through the teaching of those they teach, to enable enough of their work to be communicated to the rest of the population so that it can see a value in it and in its continued existence. Even if people in universities have in the past failed to do this and failed to appreciate the wider human significance of the world, it does not follow that they should now be expected to dilute their work or even their immediate teaching, for doing that will undermine the whole exercise, which depends on preserving and transmitting our best traditions of thought and learning at the highest level.

Nietzsche

I now have to turn to a rather more substantial set of objections to the university ideal than the set just considered. Those just considered are based on considerations external to the ideal itself, political considerations to do with expediency and an ill-thought-out egalitarianism, and are worth the amount of attention opportunism merits generally. But there is, as John Carroll has recently reminded us,[6] a deep problem inherent in the ideal itself, amounting, if we concede the point, to an incoherence. There is, indeed, something blissfully optimistic about the vision of education associated with the names of Newman, Arnold and Leavis, of education, particularly within its higher phases, as an essentially civilizing force, pulling together what has been torn apart, integrating and healing and commanding through its appeal to the best that had been thought and known and through the disciplined contact those educated might have with this best. If something like this is what we might hope for from universities properly conceived – what Newman thought of in terms of the production of *gentlemen* – then we must face up to a number of pressing problems.

First, as Leavis himself was well aware, there is the fact of increasing specialization:

The academic world is part of the contemporary world, and the university itself has been disabled for the task by the process which makes the task so urgent: the idea of liberal culture has been defeated and dissipated by advancing specialisation; and the production of specialists . . . tends to be regarded as the supreme end of the university, its *raison d'être*.[7]

Leavis wrote this in 1943, and one cannot say that matters have improved since. In his blundering and ignorant way, C. P. Snow was complaining about the same phenomenon in 1959, and part (but not all) of Leavis's invective against Snow was unjustified even on Leavis's terms. Had Leavis come by 1959 to doubt that universities could integrate despite disciplinary divisions, and to believe that specialization had gone so far that there was, in fact, no hope for any *rapproachement* between, say, physics and literature? While one sees little attempt in universities to attempt any such thing, so intent are they on specialized research and narrow teaching, often of an erroneously called vocational sort (was anyone *called* to the profession of manager or engineer?), this in itself does not invalidate the ideal.

It is interesting to see that the Secretary of State for Education is on the side of the angels on this point when he speaks about the humanities. 'A narrow scholasticism which delights in creating "more and more about less and less" can only drag the humanities down', he says.[8] I would go further at this point: for what are Newton, Darwin, Einstein and their contemporary successors such as Hawking, Adkins, Dawkins and Prigogine adumbrating, but metaphysical conceptions of the world and hence of man? These are conceptions which cannot be *justified* on empirical grounds, although they are brilliantly based on empirical evidence, far more so indeed than the cut-price metaphysics of such as Marx and Freud.[9] Where, except in a university, could there be informed, interdisciplinary discussion and evaluation of such metaphysical schemes and their meanings on a human level? As Mr Baker says, 'I hope that much of our scholarship today will remember Milton's advice to "strike high and adventure dangerously"'.[10]

Whether academics desperately fighting their corners in universities and desperately seeking to put on money-making courses of supposed, but dubious, relevance to the needs of industry and business are likely to strike high and adventure dangerously is one thing. Nietzsche's criticisms are another, and, if accepted, would show why increased specialization in universities is inevitable and that the humanizing educational ideal of Newman and Arnold is a will-o'-the-wisp. We must remember that Newman spoke from the perspective of a deep Christian and Catholic vision. As such, he could happily speak of 'the clear, calm and accurate vision and comprehension of all things, as far as the finite mind can embrace them', of referring the many pieces and types of human knowledge to 'their true place in the universal system' and of the liberally educated man possessing knowledge 'not only of things, but of their mutual and true relations'.[11] And, for Newman, the finite mind had been created by God with the power of right reason, apart from and anterior to the gift of revelation, so it could do these things even outside the Church.

Arnold, of course, wrote 'Dover Beach' as well as *Culture and Anarchy*. Leaving aside the excessive stress in that book on sweetness and light, the question which faces us today is how far culture can prevent anarchy – disintegration, dissipation, specialization – if we are really standing on Dover Beach. Nietzsche had George Eliot in mind when he wrote:

> They have got rid of the Christian God, and now feel obliged to cling all the more firmly to Christian morality: that is *English* consistency . . . the origin of English morality has been forgotten, so that the highly conditional nature of its right to exist is no longer felt. For the Englishman morality is not yet a problem . . .[12]

But he might just as well have been writing about Arnold and education, rather than about George Eliot and morality. For those of us who do see that the absence of a divine order does make the notion of a calm, clear and accurate comprehension of all things profoundly problematic, Nietzsche's challenge can cause sleepless nights. (As it did for Nietzsche himself, of course. The postmodernist conception that the most intelligent among us should somehow rejoice in intellectual anarchy, Nietzsche would have seen as the final infantile flourish of a decadent breed.)

The task of the university, as conceived by Newman and his followers, is fundamentally cultural and moral. But – and this is Nietzsche's challenge – what if the university is incapable of fulfilling that task precisely because the type of wisdom and integration of culture Newman and Arnold are looking for is not to be had? What if the intellect is unable to discover the sort of truth on which the very ideal depends? Nietzsche was convinced that it could not in either scientific or moral realms, and this set him off from *The Birth of Tragedy* onwards on the path of a ruthless deconstruction of the intellectual and his pretensions. On this path, we may identify two main conclusions: that the intellectual personality is not an admirable personality, and that the greatest moments of human history have not been brought about by intellectuals.

Indeed, the greatest moment of all, fifth-century Athens, was, in Nietzsche's opinion, actually undermined from within by the presence and activity of the archetypal intellectual, Socrates himself. In *The Birth of Tragedy*, Nietzsche draws a stunning contrast between the heroic, aristocratic morality, its heroes, its products, such as sculpture and tragedy, and the figure of Socrates, ugly, snub-nosed, physically weak, questioning, destructive, ushering in an era of the common man and the new comedy in which values are subverted and the strong are outflanked by the cleverness and rhetoric of the weak. Socrates is seen as the revenge of the snivelling, but too clever, Thersites of the *Iliad*, and there is no Odysseus to give him a good hiding. Intellectuals themselves are the weak but clever boys of the school playground who manage through their wiles to protect themselves against their moral and physical superiors. Since Socrates they have been accorded a respect and position ill-suited to their devious nature. For Nietzsche, there is no truth, and the intellectual's search for truth is a mere device, a weapon by which he can outflank the naturally strong.

A society which cherishes intellectuals will not be a cultured society or a strong society. Culture depends on myth, and the tendency of the intellectual is to undermine myth. (In *The Birth of Tragedy*, Nietzsche originally saw Wagner as the new tragedian and the new bearer of myth, but Nietzsche was an intellectual and could not bear it when Wagner started to believe all this.) Technology and civilization are the result of intellectuals and their work, along with comfort, rationality, democracy, mediocrity. As John Carroll points out in his article, the Weberian technical specialist subserving *Zweckrationalität* and the university of specialists is the logical consequence of all this. Our society is, no doubt, the most comfortable, most technically advanced, most utilitarian, most rational there has ever been; the most civilized but almost completely lacking in culture, and certainly lacking in a sustaining myth. In terms of cultural achievement, our time is not to be compared with Periclean Athens or Augustan Rome or Medici Florence or Elizabethan England or seventeenth-century France, all eras deeply offensive to the democratic spirit, all, in Nietzsche's sense, cultures inspired by aristocratic myth rather than by the values of civilization, comfort, egalitarianism and a self-serving and critical intellectualism.

If there is anything in Nietzsche's typology of the intellectual, then one is liable to find modern universities stocked with two types of people. First there will be the technicians of the bureaucratic society, applied scientists, engineers, trainers of management. These will not necessarily be intellectuals in Nietzsche's sense, and perhaps will, at least from a professional point of view, have no interest in questions of culture and civilization. Then there will be the intellectuals proper: those in society attracted to the university because of the scope it gives to their particular talents for cleverness, rationalization and scepticism. In this context, as John Carroll comments,

> a university will always be close to the edge of doing more harm than good, attracting as it does, in both its teachers and its students, the members of society with their instincts most under strain, the most wrought, tense, inhibited and intelligent individuals. It doesn't take much to turn such people to malice, with a fervent bitter drive to destroy whatever is good. In such a climate only the most vigilant maintenance of the authority and direction of the institution will check the potential for rancour and grandiose pedantry from breaking out.[13]

To which anyone who has ever attended a meeting of a university faculty or senate can only nod assent. And even if we look to that very part of the university which professes to uphold the moral decencies against both technicism and New Leftist suspicion of the very notion of legitimacy – the Leavisite English department – we actually find nothing of the sort, but only self-righteousness, pettiness and malice, as Carroll puts it.

The Nietzsche–Carroll view of the university intellectual has more than a modicum of truth in it as descriptive phenomenology. Apart from anything else, university humanities departments are filled with people who actually agree with Nietzsche in substance, who profess not to believe in truth or any values not entirely circumscribed by the limitations of time and place. Although their heroes might be Frantz Fanon or Michel Foucault rather than Cesare Borgia or

Lorenzo de' Medici, they agree with Nietzsche in seeing claims to knowledge and moral rectitude as simply the masks of power. They see the task of thought as the stripping away of such masks, in order to replace existing power with some other form of power (usually completely underdescribed).

But we should not accept the Nietzschean epistemology, and in universities we have a duty to resist it if our faith is good. While human beings and their judgements are indeed initially products of historical circumstance, they, as individuals, have self-consciousness and powers of reflection by which they can step outside their inheritance and their community. These powers allow us to step outside the narrowness of our own time and to seek a more universal truth and reason. Nietzsche himself actually tried to do this in claiming that knowledge and reason were but the masks of power; but this claim was a claim to know and based on reasons (of a sort) and so self-destructs.

In the absence of an underlying divine order, the task of seeking the universal in the particular is immensely hard. The irresponsibility of deconstruction is far easier, and more fun. But it is only the establishment and transmission of some sort of canon of the best that has been thought and known, that can prevent the anarchy and cultural fragmentation Arnold feared. Our historically transcendent powers of thought and reflection do allow us to do this. The task is easier in the natural sciences where, whatever critics might say, there is in the end the bar of an impartial nature at which our theories and speculations have to stand. But the task is more urgent in the humanities, that area of enquiry in which we explore what we are and what we might become. We in universities have to show by our work and teaching that judgements in this area are neither masks for power structures nor determinable solely by consumer choice. Whatever the personal faults of Leavis and his followers, and it is easy to laugh at them, there is still something right and urgent in their vision of the essential role of the university. If universities are to have any significant role in the 1990s, it must be the Leavisite one of bringing specialist knowledge into effective relation with informed general intelligence, humane culture, social conscience and political will.[14] But first we have to demonstrate the legitimacy of our specialist knowledge, particularly in the humanities, against the onslaughts of Nietzsche and his present-day followers.

Notes

1 John Henry Newman, *The Idea of a University*, Longman Green, London, 1929 edition (originally published in 1852).
2 F. R. Leavis, *Education and the University*, Cambridge University Press, 1979, p. 24.
3 Newman, *The Idea of a University*, Discourse VI, part 6, p. 139.
4 Ibid.
5 Socrates, *Phaedrus*, 274C–275B.
6 John Carroll, 'The Post-Humanist University: Three Theses', *Salisbury Review*, December 1988, pp. 20–5.
7 Leavis, *Education*, p. 35.

8 Kenneth Baker, 'The Place of the Humanities', speech delivered to the British Academy, 7 July 1988.

9 Cf A. O'Hear, *Element of Fire*, Routledge, 1988, Ch. 3, on the balance in science between empiricism and metaphysics. The whole book attempts to explore the relationship between the sciences and humanities.

10 Baker, 'The Place of the Humanities'. As this piece is appearing in a book, which may have some political significance, I suppose that one should ask how far the policies for higher education we see these days actually permit the sort of university and the sort of humanities work in universities Mr Baker is looking for. Or rather, I suppose, Mr Baker should ask himself that question.

11 Newman, *The Idea of a University*, pp. 134, 137.

12 F. Nietzsche, *Twilight of the Idols*, Penguin, 1968, pp. 69–70 (originally published in 1889).

13 Carroll, 'The Post-Humanist University', p. 25.

14 Cf. Leavis, *Education*, p. 24.

3

Access and Standards: An Unresolved (and Unresolvable?) Debate

Leslie Wagner

It began with Robbins and the skirmishing has continued ever since. Does the expansion of higher education bring with it a lowering of standards? For Robbins the answer was clearly in the negative and the issue was addressed directly in the Committee's report:

> It is sometimes argued that growth in the number of those able to benefit from higher education is something that is likely to be limited in the foreseeable future by biological factors. But we believe that it is highly misleading to suppose that one can determine an upper limit to the number of people who could benefit from higher education, given favourable circumstances . . . We think there is no risk that within the next twenty years the growth in the proportion of young people with qualifications and aptitudes suitable for entry to higher education will be restrained by a shortage of potential ability.[1]

The statistics, at one level, bear out Robbins's conclusions. In 1962 there were just under 200,000 home students in full-time higher education, representing some 8.5 per cent of the 18-year-old age group. By 1987 the figure had risen to well in excess of 500,000 which represented more than 14 per cent of the age group.

But to those who believe 'more means worse' rather than 'more means different', or even 'more means better', these are unconvincing statistics. For the notion of 'standards' is so imprecise that it can be argued that if more are reaching the standard then it is the standard itself which has been debased. If a greater percentage of the age group are passing A levels, this cannot be because schooling has improved – all our prejudices tell us otherwise – but because the exam is easier. If more students are successfully completing a course of higher education, this is not because the quality of students has improved but because the quality of the course has deteriorated. Once there is a fixed point of reference all other variables must adjust to it.

This attitude to standards in higher education is a prime example of a closed system of belief. I remember many years ago as an undergraduate having this explained to me in terms of a person who is convinced he is dead. No amount of argument will convince him that he is not dead. Eventually he is asked 'Do dead men bleed?' He pauses and considers the matter and agreed that dead men do not bleed. Whereupon a pin is produced, his thumb is pricked and a small amount of blood spurts out. 'There you are,' he is told, 'you are not dead.' The man looks with amazement at his thumb and eventually exclaims. 'Good Lord, dead men do bleed!'

So, if you believe that dead men do bleed, nothing that is written here will convince you otherwise.

Entry standards

The normal entry requirement for higher education for over 30 years has been performance in the Advanced level of the General Certificate of Education. The minimum requirement for entry to a degree course is a pass in two subjects and, for a Higher National Diploma course, a pass in one subject. It is curious that this condition is nowhere part of any governmental regulation but, rather, has been introduced by the higher education institutions themselves.

The A level still dominates entry to higher education, remaining bloody but unbowed despite many attacks, the latest of which is the Higginson Report.[2] At the beginning of the 1980s some 90 per cent of those obtaining university degrees, and close to 75 per cent of those obtaining CNAA degrees, had two or more A levels on entry.

It is difficult to see how an argument can be sustained that 'standards' of A level performance have fallen as the numbers of those obtaining that standard have risen. The notion of a standard can be interpreted in two ways. It can measure either an absolute level of knowledge and intellectual understanding of a subject and/or a rate of change between a previous and a new level of knowledge and understanding. The concept can best be described with the aid of a graph.[3] In Figure 3.1 (which is not as complicated as it looks), particular

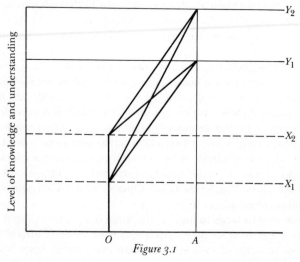

Figure 3.1

levels of knowledge and understanding are identified on the vertical axis as X and Y with four absolute levels shown as X_1, X_2, Y_1 and Y_2. On the horizontal axis particular qualifications which might be depicted as O and A levels are shown. Suppose the absolute level attained by an O level in a subject (or, to be entirely modern, a GCSE) is given by the point OX_1, and the absolute level attained by an A level shown by the point AY_1. The rate of change or standard of learning gain is shown by the slope of the line between these two points.

Now, suppose the level of knowledge required for success at A level is raised to Y_2. Clearly the absolute standard has risen and if the O level remains at X_1 then the rate of learning gain required has also risen. The slope from OX_1 to AY_2 is steeper. If, however, the starting point has also risen (to OX_2), the slope of learning gain may be flatter. Standards require both a measure of absolute levels and of rates of change.

A third variable of time can also be introduced. This has not been shown in Figure 3.1 because it would make the diagram too complex. However, it might be felt that standards of learning gain also depend on time. So an A level gained in two years might be distinguished from an A level gained in three years. The latter would be measured further along the horizontal axis so that while the absolute level reached might be the same the slope of the rate of change of learning gain would be more gentle.

All the anecdotal evidence would seem to support the argument that standards of entry to higher education in both absolute and rate of change terms have risen over the past two decades. The extension of the boundaries of knowledge and understanding at the highest levels have had their impact lower down. It is commonplace to find concepts which a decade or two ago were part of a Masters degree course now being taught in the second or third year of an undergraduate programme and, as part of this process, concepts and skills which were central to undergraduate teaching now featuring as part of an A-level course. There can be little doubt that, in terms of absolute levels of knowledge and understanding, the standards required for A-level success have increased over the last two decades. In terms of Figure 3.1, we have moved from Y_1 to Y_2.

What about rate of change? Here the anecdotal evidence is more diffuse but still convincing. The pressure of the A-level syllabus will have had its cascade effect on the O-level syllabus so that it is quite likely that the knowledge and understanding base of this examination has also risen over the last two decades. On the other hand, 'standards' of those emerging from the school system with or without this qualification are increasingly criticized. In large part, these criticisms and the counter arguments seem to stem from very different notions of what might be expected as a measure of achievement, which in turn reflects distinct value systems. It is difficult to see how they might be objectively ranked but what emerges from the confused debate about O levels is that any increase in absolute levels over the past two decades is unlikely to have matched that achieved by A levels. So the rate of change of standards has, if anything, steepened over the period. Standards have improved in both absolute and relative terms.

Entry standards and access

The substantial increase in those obtaining the traditional qualifications for entry to higher education does not seem to have been accompanied by any lowering of standards. Indeed, as the analysis in the previous section has shown, the opposite is the more likely case. However, the insistence on this standard as the basis of entry to higher education has had a significant impact on access.

The present curriculum and structure of the GCE A level has come under increasing attack as more and more out of place in the changing pattern of UK higher education. Some 25 years ago the overwhelming majority of under-graduate students took single or joint honours in one or two subjects. The model followed was of a progression through increasing specialization, from the early through middle years of secondary schooling on to the later years of schooling into higher education. To study a science or arts subject to single honours level required its study at A level. The absolute level of knowledge required implied that only three subjects could be studied in total and the single-mindedness of the higher education syllabus suggested that the chosen subject should be supported by the study of cognate areas. To ensure an adequate preparation for A level, some specialization was required at O level. And so it came to pass that specialization began at the age of 13 or 14.

One result has been an acute shortage of applicants for mathematics, engineering and the sciences. This in turn has forced academics to review the syllabus requirements and their teaching methods for these courses, to accommodate entrants with less specialized knowledge. In both sciences and arts, single and joint honours are being joined by more unusual combinations of subjects and more general and less specialist-based courses.

This change at the higher levels of education is being accompanied by movement at the other end with the replacement of O levels by the GCSE. While single subjects are retained, the skills and assessment base are much broader in range. The Higginson Report recognized that this pincer movement made the A level look more and more redundant, reflecting neither the developments going on below or above it.[4] But the government thought otherwise and, for the time being, the A level remains like some beached whale, unresponsive to what precedes it and increasingly irrelevant to what follows it.

While it remains, however, it will exert its baneful influence on access, acting as a barrier to further academic progress for a large group of 16-year-olds, and particularly those from working-class homes. While improved GCSE attainment might encourage some of those students to carry on, the Eiger face impact of the unchanging A level will remain.

It is a curious fact of the UK and UK attitude to access that while in the United States the compensation for poor schooling and underachievement is sought immediately, in remedial programmes in high school and freshman year in college, in the United Kingdom the major effort in this direction occurs some years later. When US educators talk of access for blacks, other ethnic groups, women and lower social groups, they think first of teenagers and devote their energies and resources to reform of the schooling system to provide immediate improvement and enable pupils to continue into higher education.

In the United Kingdom our rigid structures mean that access routes to higher education take place outside the schooling system and apply to adults rather than teenagers. We do not seek to correct the effects of schooling immediately. Rather, we wait until the alienation has weakened through the confused years (and confusing education and training system) of the late teens. As people move into their twenties, maturity, family responsibility and career needs come to the forefront and they become more susceptible to the benefits to be obtained by the qualifications provided by the higher education experience.

Access routes

Some of these mature students will follow the traditional route and return to college to study A levels. A survey at the beginning of the 1980s showed that 95 per cent of mature students in universities and 83 per cent of those in polytechnics had qualifications at A level or above. Even 77 per cent of Open University students were in this category.

Increasingly during the 1980s, specially-designed access courses (typically, one year full-time) have been introduced to offer mature students a non-traditional route into higher education. The first such courses began in 1978 and the 1987 White Paper[5] recognizes such courses as one of the three entry routes into higher education, the other two being A levels and vocational qualifications such as the Ordinary National Diploma.

Woodrow identifies three characteristics of access courses.[6] The first is that they are targeted towards groups traditionally underrepresented in higher education. For example, some are for women only or for particular ethnic groups. A second characteristic is that they are delivered by a process of collaboration between further education and higher education institutions. Typically, the course will take place in the further education institution but be jointly developed, delivered and monitored by staff in both institutions. A final characteristic is that they offer clear progression, not just a preparation for, but a route into higher education. Sometimes this progression is linked to a particular course in higher education; on other occasions it provides a more general access.

The number of access courses is now well over 400 and continuing to rise. Following the 1987 White Paper, and at the invitation of the Department of Education and Science, the Council for National Academic Awards (CNAA) is putting in place a national system of recognition for the accreditation of such courses. They are going to remain an increasing part of the landscape of higher education entry in the 1990s. They offer a very different entry standard from that provided by A levels, seemingly well suited to their particular client group. Whether this results in a fall in *entry* standards is an arid debate. It is time for the debate to move on to the issue of standards in higher education itself.

Higher education standards

Figure 3.1 can be applied to the question of standards within higher education itself. Instead of the horizontal lines representing O and A levels, they can now represent A levels or, more generally, entry standards and first-degree level. The gradient of the slope would then represent what has been termed the 'value added' by the higher education experience; the steeper the slope, the greater the value added.

So what can be said about the changing standards of the higher education output? Quite a lot, but nothing very precise. In terms of absolute level, it can be argued that the increase in levels of knowledge and skill required at A level has been matched by a similar upgrading at first-degree level. Final-year students in general now complete their studies at a higher level of complexity than a generation ago, if only to reflect the advancement of knowledge over that period.

However, the counter-view, similarly plausible, is that this increased complexity covers a narrower range. Students know more and more about less and less. Standards have neither improved nor declined, it is argued. They simply reflect a different measurement. Indeed, a similar argument is used by those who defend the more general courses now increasingly prevalent in higher education in which students perhaps know less and less about more and more. These do not imply, they argue, a lowering of standards but a different form of measurement.

An appeal to external valuation also yields contradictory results. In terms of academic and professional competence, standards seem to have risen. The increasing numbers with first-class honours does not seem to have led to any suggestion that the standard of that award has fallen. On the contrary, those responsible for research bemoan the lack of opportunities for the many first-class researchers available. Similarly, the increase in number of those whose degree qualifications make them eligible for exemption from professional examination has not led to any suggestion that the professional bodies are lowering their standards. On the contrary, in some professional areas there is sharp criticism that, by maintaining outdated views of what is required for professional exemption, the profession is unnecessarily excluding many worthwhile candidates.

Employers, on the other hand, seem to have had long-standing criticisms of the higher education experience as a preparation for work. This was reflected, for example, in the evidence of the Confederation of British Industry to the inquiry of the House of Commons Education, Science and Arts Committee in 1980, and, more recently, in the work undertaken by Boys *et al.*[7] However, a study of these views indicates that they are a criticism not of declining standards but of the criteria by which such standards are measured. For what employers are complaining about is that higher education concentrates too much on subject knowledge – the essence of the academic criterion of standards – and too little on what has become known as 'transferable personal skills'. The two need not be incompatible but, if they are, the clear message from employers is that they would prefer a little less specialist subject knowledge, which in large part they do not need, and a little more numeracy, literacy, communication, teamwork and leadership skills, which they do need. What we have here is a plea for different rather than lower standards.

Well, if the expansion of A-level qualified students has not weakened standards, the same cannot surely be said for the increasing numbers coming in without this traditional qualification. Not so, according to a major survey undertaken by the CNAA to study the relationship between entry qualifications and degree performance. The survey covered more than 17,000 honours degree graduates from the CNAA in 1983. As reported earlier, over a quarter of these did not have at least two A levels when they entered and, in total, some 11.5 per cent came with what the CNAA regards as non-standard entry.[8] To quote the report which was issued following the study: 'Students within the non-standard entry categories fare no worse than the other groups of entrants. Indeed, when entry qualifications of similar level are grouped together it is seen that the non-standard entrants, on average, fare a little better than other groups.'[9] The criterion of performance used in the analysis is the percentage of entrants getting a first or upper second. With non-standard entrants 39.5 per cent come into this category while for those with two A levels the figure is 38.3 per cent. Of course, these are averages for large cohorts. The higher scoring A-level students achieve a much higher percentage of firsts and upper seconds but there is no point of comparison. By definition, it is not possible in any formal sense to identify the 'better' non-standard students on entry.

One final argument is left to those who persist with the view that more must mean worse: the differentiation of degrees from different institutions. Thus, Oxbridge is better than Redbrick, which is better than New, which is better than ex-CAT, which is better than Polytechnic. A degree is a degree is a degree, but not quite. By this argument, the title might be the same but the standard is not.

Such evidence as exists for this view relates to the different A-level entry scores of students at different institutions. Higher input must mean higher output. Yes, but . . . Over the system as a whole there is no evidence that A-level scores have deteriorated as numbers have increased, and it has been shown that non-standard entrants perform marginally better than the average of A-level students. Moreover, there is in place a system of external examiners (except, curiously, at Oxbridge) to ensure comparability of standards of final degree awards. Moreover, the polytechnics provide a standard CNAA degree which, until recently, required detailed external scrutiny in which university academics played a major role. And they are also subject to the regular supervision of Her Majesty's Inspectorate. The academic standards of UK higher education are probably subject to more rigorous internal and external scrutiny than any comparable system in Western Europe or the United States.

In truth, the attack on differential standards in different institutions is necessary and indeed vital to those who wish to maintain the status quo. If it cannot be sustained, the elitist world is damned. For if a first at some universities, which only accept students with 12 or more points at A level, is the same as a first at a polytechnic which accepts entrants with much lower A-level scores and with non-standard qualifications, how can the former justify its existence, or at least its more substantial resourcing? In terms of Figure 3.1, if the end level is the same but the starting point is much lower, the slope has been steeper and the value added much greater.

Conclusion

We have arrived at the nub of the whole exercise. The argument that wider access leads to lower standards is essential to maintain the privileges of the academic elite. And the notion of what is meant by 'standards' and whether we are referring to 'adequate' or 'high' is so vague that the word is capable of a range of meanings to suit any argument. The issue will never be resolved because whenever evidence is provided to refute the proposition that access leads to lower standards, the meaning of 'standards' will be redefined.

We enter the 1990s with a strong political wind behind the policy of wider access. The Secretary of State for Education and Science has called for a participation rate of 20 per cent by 1995 going up to 30 per cent into the next century,[10] seemingly without any concern for its effect on standards. That message is an encouraging one for those who wish to widen the opportunities in higher education for young people and adults. But all the other messages are in the opposite direction. It is those who restrict access by accepting only students with the highest traditional qualifications which receive the status, prestige, honours and resources. It is still accepted implicitly, and occasionally stated explicitly, that those institutions who widen access only do so because they cannot attract the more traditionally qualified students. Access is seen as necessary to fill empty places, not as a deliberate choice of discrimination in favour of certain types of students. The argument that certain institutions widen access because they want to, rather than because they need to, is simply disbelieved.

The exclusivist culture of higher education, indeed of our whole society, bites deep into its soul. To widen is to weaken. For all the fine words, access is not only not part of that culture, but a threat to its very existence. And that is why the debate over standards will continue for evermore.

Notes

1 Committee on Higher Education, *Higher Education. Report of the Committee under the Chairmanship of Lord Robbins*, Cmnd 2154, HMSO, 1963, pp. 49, 54.
2 Department of Education and Science, *Advancing A Levels*, HMSO, 1988.
3 I am indebted to a conversation with Sir Hermann Bondi which stimulated my thoughts in this direction. The responsibility for this analysis, however, is entirely my own.
4 DES, *Advancing A Levels*, p. 9.
5 DES, *Higher Education: Meeting the Challenge*, Cm 114, HMSO, 1987.

6 M. Woodrow, 'The Access Route to Higher Education', *Higher Education Quarterly*, vol. 42, no. 4, Autumn 1988.

7 Confederation of British Industry, *Minutes of Evidence – Education, Science and Arts Committee. The Funding and Organisation of Courses in Higher Education*, House of Commons Paper 363-x, Session 1979–80, p. 329. C. Boys *et al.*, *Higher Education and the Preparation for Work*, Jessica Kingsley, 1989.

8 This is covered by the following categories: up to 5 O levels; 1 A level; City & Guilds; or what the CNAA terms 'exceptional admissions', that is, no formal qualifications.

9 T. Bourner and M. Hamed, *Entry Qualifications and Degree Performance*, CNAA Development Services, Publication no. 10, 1987.

10 'Baker's Vision for the Next 25 Years', *Times Higher Education Supplement*, 13 January 1989, p. 7.

4

The Pattern, Range and Purpose of Higher Education: A Moral Perspective

Kenneth Wilson

Any system of education will need to be tested against a wide variety of criteria; higher education no less than the school system must expect to be included. Indeed, accountability should be welcomed by any institution which intends by its work to offer public services: higher education is no exception. This is not, of course, to threaten academic freedom but a condition of its healthy continuation and development. It was Karl Jaspers who wrote of an academic institution:

> The university is a community of scholars and students engaged in the task of seeking truth. It derives its autonomy from the idea of academic freedom, a privilege granted to it by state and society which entails the obligation to teach truth in defiance of all internal and external attempts to curtail it.[1]

Whatever we make of the expression 'to teach truth' we have some understanding which we regard as valuable and to which we would want to be committed, but by the same token we will want to be assured that in the context of teaching truth certain other benefits are also assured. As Derek Bok said, 'the cloistered university could probably exist only at a heavy cost to the quality of professional education, applied research, social criticism, and expert advice – activities that are all important to our society'.[2] On occasions some of the services offered may overlap with and should be superseded by those offered by other agencies in order to clarify the distinctive roles of academic institutions, but a higher education which is not committed to the service of the community in its teaching, researching and provision of educational opportunity to the wider society will be failing in its duty and falling short of its own best aspirations.

And if the higher education system regards this as a new example of the meddlesome society, that on the whole betrays a singular lack of historical perspective on the development of the system. We have always been subject to judgement and influence from institutions outside ourselves. The burgeoning of the universities in medieval Europe was itself a response to the needs of the expanding urban life and the particular demands of the type of society coming consequentially into existence which required a more practical and businesslike approach to the courses on offer if the tasks involved in commerce, state and church were to be undertaken by the products of the system. A recent book on the early history of Oxford and Cambridge universities refers to the competition amongst tutors for students and, it should be said (sadly!), the comparative depression of the fees which could be demanded by arts tutors.[3] *Plus ça change, plus c'est la même chose.* We likewise experience pressures from many directions, and need to learn to respond to the opportunities given us and the demands made of us; far from being a necessary undermining of the academic freedom we quite rightly cherish, the satisfaction of these interests is the necessary condition of its development.

The nineteenth and twentieth centuries have seen the huge expansion of higher education, and the demands of our changing society combined with the increase in population (from 5 billion in 1987 to 8 billion in 2022), the increasing rate of social and technical development and a growing complexity in the issues clamouring for attention, suggest that the future is likely to see yet further exponential growth in higher education. At a time of nostalgic reference to a mythical past uncontaminated by external pressure, or the demand for relevance, the ideals of those who discussed the future of higher education in the nineteenth century, or its possibility and importance, are interesting. Perhaps most famous of all is John Henry Newman, whose work *The Idea of a University*, led his most recent editor, I. T. Ker, to claim that all subsequent writing on university education is a series of footnotes to Newman's lectures and essays.[4] It was Newman who declared:

> If then a practical end must be assigned to a University course, I say it is that of training good members of society. Its art is the art of social life, and its end is fitness for the world. . . . [It is not] content . . . with forming the critic or the experimentalist, the economist or the engineer, though such too it includes within its scope. But a University training is the great ordinary means to a great but ordinary end; it aims at raising the intellectual tone of society, at cultivating the public mind, at purifying the national taste, at supplying true principles to popular enthusiasm and fixed aims to popular aspiration, at giving enlargement and sobriety to the ideas of the age, at facilitating the exercise of political power, and refining the intercourse of private life. It is the education which gives a man a clear conscious view of his own opinions and judgements, a truth in developing them, an eloquence in expressing them, and a force in urging them.[5]

There is no isolationism in this ambitious plea, for the education implicit in higher education has as its end the improvement of society, the fulfilment of the individual and the development of that moral insight which brings about the educated community in which rational judgement and mutual respect lead to appropriate, acceptable and morally defensible decisions.

These are not isolated ideals, even if their English style, it has to be admitted, is paramount. Take Henry Tappan, for example, formerly Professor of Philosophy at the University of New York, later President of the University of Michigan, who went to Europe and was inspired by the German university system to write a notable criticism of higher education in the United States which he published in 1851 under the title *University Education*. He saw an academic institution as providing all the physical resources of learning on which a self-motivated student might draw, with lectures as conversation introducing them to enquiries not yet published, and with every facility for experiment and reflection. He continues:

> Universities may, indeed, make learned men; but their best commendation is given when it can be said of them, that furnishing the material and appliances of learning, setting the examples in their professors and gradu-ates, breathing the spirit of scholarship in all that pertains to them, they inspire men, by the self-creative force of study and thought, to make themselves both learned and wise, and thus ready to put their hand to every great and good work, whether of science, of religion, or of the state.[6]

The purposes of higher education in both these reflections are theoretical and practical, private and public, personal and social, and above all moral. This latter purpose we neglect at our peril. This range of purposes indicates the appropriateness of looking at the output of higher education in so far as it succeeds or fails to meet the demands of the market. It is right that some students study history and indeed do research in it, but wrong that too many should. We as a society need doctors, too, and physicists and ecologists. And while it would be good to be able to view our higher education system as if it fulfilled Newman's hope that it would prepare every student 'to fill any post with credit, and to master any subject with facility',[7] our specialist sixth-form curriculum, combined with the continuing specialism of our first-degree pro-gramme (a specialism partly made necessary by the comparatively low pro-portion of our 18-year-olds who enter higher education), mean that this is not so. Attention has to be given to the recruitment patterns in subject areas. We know the difficulties, and maybe impossibilities in some cases, but it has to be attempted in the short term. In the longer term, of course, one anticipates much change as a result of the large increase in those involved in higher education.

There will also need to be attention to the effectiveness of the learning process, which will be related to its efficiency. At a time of diminishing resources, the cry of value for money will be heard long and clear. This will also be directed at research. Low levels of completion by research students on doctoral pro-grammes may have many explanations, but it is entirely reasonable that they should be investigated and compared. Indeed, the ability of institutions and departments to pick up research money will itself be a matter of objective interest, together with the range of the investigations in progress and their apparent relevance and usefulness. Not everything is right with this approach and much will depend on the style if it is to be of actual use. We do not want to threaten the academic freedom, on the one hand, while on the other we want as a society to be sure that at a time of scarce resources enough of them are going to support investigation into areas of immediate and public concern.

Furthermore, higher education needs to be as familiar with the schools, their management, curriculum and ideals as with the requirements of employers both public and private, if the courses are to be both teachable and appropriate. To pretend that one occupies that no man's land between the discipline of school and the responsibilities of the market as if one had no real link with either is foolish arrogance. Openness to influence from both these potentially collaborative social structures is crucial for our well-being; we have been too anxious on occasions to provide advice with a non-returnable label. Above all, we should know that institutions, like individuals and societies, only have the opportunity to teach in so far as they are seen to be willing to learn.

But all these things are coming to be accepted. There is one other dimension to the process of education which we offer, namely the moral, which is less debated, indeed on which we seem more than a little coy. It is understandable; after all, the Latey Report recommended the reduction of the age of majority to 18 years of age from the previous 21, and the removal at a stroke of any role which an institution or individual might formerly have been required to undertake *in loco parentis*.[8] But such a view is for me an abrogation of responsibility for reasons which are bound up with the reasonableness of the criteria briefly reviewed above. It is easy for us to avoid it because, as we say, it does not obviously figure on the bottom line; indeed, it does not exist as a category at all either in the budget or in the audited accounts. Yet it is abundantly clear to employers that loyalty, courage, optimism and the sheer ability to work hard as a member of a team are as important as mere possession of knowledge or the acquisition of skills. Indeed, many selection processes are concerned with identifying just these sorts of qualities. And all of them require that the student be given the opportunity to gain a knowledge of himself or herself; without this personal insight, the knowledge and skills may be wasted. On a value-for-money basis, that is a poor return.

The remainder of this essay is concerned with developing this point and drawing out some of the implications. The preliminary point is to dissociate this from the counselling services, careers advice and contributions made by the students' union and the other student societies. These services are necessary. There will be many occasions from time to time when a student will require the sort of professional conversation which a trained counsellor can offer and a careers advisory service will be necessary whatever the burgeoning job market which is envisaged for graduates, or perhaps because of it. And a students' union which is not supportive and committed to the personal well-being of its members is hardly worth having. But these services do not singly or together supply the need which is here identified. For one thing, they do not themselves embody and express the commitment of the institution to encouraging the personal maturity of students. A counselling service will necessarily be confidential, and may even, therefore, best be provided by an external agency; a careers service has a specific focus and a students' union by definition does not involve the academic staff. In contrast, what is required is the public acceptance of responsibility on the part of the academic institution itself for the quality of the product as a whole: to suggest that this can be carried out by another service or by contracting out is to fail to see the point. The educational experience, planned and accidental, with which students are engaged must be such as to provide consciously for them; institutional management strategies must be such as to make them matters of central discussion for which it can be seen to be accepting responsibility.

The reasonableness of this expectation is patent. In educating a doctor one wants to know that technical competence and scientific knowledge are such as to be sufficient for him or her to enter happily into the language of judgement which the profession uses. But one also needs to be sure that there is adequate awareness of what it is to be a person, since it is the patient's understanding and co-operation that will be crucial for the success of long-term health in most cases. Furthermore, the availability of new techniques through the application of advances in scientific enquiry make it vital that a doctor has a sensitivity to moral issues, if all parties in a treatment process are to feel content with what is going on. Society at large has to feel content with the care the medical profession offers on its behalf. A sense of oneself, a knowledge that one can accept responsibility for one's knowledge, rather than simply turning it into a support for power which is its own justification, is essential.

It may be thought that the easy example of the medical profession is simply the exception that proves the rule. Nothing could be further from the truth. The study of history or botany, the pursuit of enquiry in physics or in classical archaeology, all alike offer roads to self-knowledge. Any discipline could. The point is, however, that it will only actually do so if it is the policy of the institution to ensure that it does. One might suggest that those general disciplines of study where the majority of students are 'gaining an education' are precisely the ones where special attention should be directed, since the companies and public services which seek to employ their successful graduates will be particularly concerned with what the subject has done for the student, as opposed to what the student literally remembers of what he or she has been taught. In vocationally directed courses, where most of the information re-quired is of direct interest to the prospective employer, there is at least something to be grasped, though, as I have said, the potential of the person for professional responsibility will be equally important.

It would be well if at this stage I pointed out that I was not looking for the development of a student-centred higher education, when at long last in the schools we were moving away from the assumption that all teaching and learning was pupil-centred. Both views suffer from the misapprehension that one can be done effectively without the other. We cannot have effective child-centred learning if there is not equal attention given to the content and subject mix of the curriculum: with equal, and no more, emphasis, I wish to say that in higher education exclusive concentration on research, learning and teaching without reference to the quality of the person who will have responsi-bility for using the knowledge and skills which we enable him or her to acquire is unreasonable. We are responsible and should accept the fact.

Of course it is difficult. Of that there can be no doubt. But since it appears, despite any protestations to the contrary, that we for the most part find ourselves paradoxically making judgements on the personal qualities of students in the references we write, it would be well to look formally and constructively at the ways in which we might not only better equip ourselves to make the judgements, but offer stimulus to students for their personal maturity. It is difficult and nothing can be or should be prescriptive. Nevertheless, there are four contexts in which discussion might take matters further.

The role of a general curriculum

The question of a general curriculum is a vexed one. Time was when every student in a Scottish university studied moral philosophy and in particular read the words of David Hume. In its early days the University of Keele offered a cross-faculty foundation course involving a common programme of study including Plato's *Republic*. The American commitment to general education is well known and attempts have been made to revive the tradition, most notably at Harvard, since the Vietnam War and the student revolts of the late 1960s led everyone involved in education down the route marked 'relevance' to the exclusion of general or personal education.

The UK situation is different since, latterly at least, our regard for specialism has been greater than our commitment to education. However, we did at one time assume the moral high ground and argue for the relevance, not simply the interest, of a well-stocked mind. On this basis, who is to know what at some time or other may be of direct professional use to a lawyer and enable him to understand a case whose legal ramifications may otherwise have been missed or even rejected? It may be that a case involves knowledge of building practices, or appropriate pedagogy for deaf children, or the classification of renaissance art. A manager who is to get the best results from his team could have use for almost any realm of discourse in order to interpret a target, or to get an agreement properly understood. And a teacher who fails to see that the development of a historical understanding may imply knowledge of technology or accounting practice simply operates within too limited a perspective. So we may be able to begin a move towards a 'general education' by the ways in which through teaching and interpreting our own disciplines we are able to place them in relation to and in mutual dependence upon other areas of enquiry.

But that is not all. A general ability to see what we know in intellectual context so that we can draw on a range of specialisms in dealing with problems is obviously crucial; attending to the moral character which enables students to accept responsibility for their knowledge is another thing. While the first matter is a straightforward curriculum question, the latter has other dimensions. It would be worthwhile raising again the question of further moral enquiry in higher education. Could we devise a programme which would not only be seen to be relevant and teachable, but which could be offered interestingly and welcomed by students? It would have many advantages if we could, since in principle it might contribute powerfully to the development of an educated society with a common set of languages of discourse with which to debate and in which to decide the public issues of the day. The creation of such a community would be a valuable aim for any system of higher education to adopt; it is one to which I turn briefly again in the final section.

But even a widening awareness of a common set of languages of enquiry, were a general course to provide it, would be insufficient. We are talking of a student's ability to deal with peers, the ability to cope with failure, the willingness to accept responsibility, the appreciation of loyalty, the determination to succeed, the capacity to be a colleague. And these are matters of the hidden curriculum as much as they are matters of anything else. How can we determine that appearances matter, when as institutions we appear to put no resources into maintaining and developing standards? How can we command colleagueship as of fundamental value, if in the management of the institution all communication seems to be one-way? How can we argue the acceptance of responsibility if there is in the institution as a whole no public accepted procedure for judging accountability? The style and ethos of the institution as a whole express the moral coherence and perception of what is involved in being responsible for knowledge and skill.

There is a physical aspect to the hidden curriculum, too, which is presented by the priorities which are seen to dominate the decisions about the allocation of resources. In an institution which is committed to research, teaching and learning, it is clear that priorities are in one sense already determined. However, it is not so clear what these areas of work should be taken to include. Certainly in times of financial stringency their delimitation is likely to be so closely interpreted as to squeeze out a great deal of what nourishes the human ability to engage in them, or to be affected by them. The maintenance of buildings, the arrangement of the physical structures which constitute the institution, the development of library and learning resources, the encouragement of communication, and all those subtle and unaccessible arrangements, personal, public, intellectual and social, which make for the realities of academic community and provide the ambience of intellectual enquiry; all these tend to be subservient to a presumed higher purpose, whereas in my judgement they are essential for the continuous development of the institution's work.

Even more generally, and with regard to the higher education system as a whole, the overall perceived purpose will be a substantial element on the hidden curriculum. Have we at heart the provision of graduates to enhance the general well-being of society or the personal education of students who can take their education and make a good living out of it? This is a false question – who can know the motives of those with whom we are engaged, or indeed our own motives for that matter? Yet as I have suggested above, it should be a matter of concern for us. But it will only be seen to be a matter of concern if we ourselves bring judgement to bear upon the nature and purpose of our work which is seen publicly to have a moral dimension. Perhaps we should consider the source of money before accepting it; perhaps research contracts are not all of equal merit provided only that they pay; perhaps the teaching quality of the staff should be given a higher prominence than their research record; perhaps we should make sure that the general moral questions which face the human race are given some sort of prominence in the world of enquiry which we set for ourselves.

None of this will happen if we have no image of ourselves, no language of integrity from which to speak, no moral perception of our role. Simply to take our style of operation from elsewhere, as if survival in a competitive world was all that mattered, is to neglect the fact that it is a responsibility of the educated community to set the agenda and provide the universe of discourse. And given the fact that higher education provides for the most part 'the educated community', or is at least the major influence upon it, we have a responsibility to take that work with moral seriousness. In one sense it is important that the students for whose future we are responsible should come to feel themselves part of an academic community which is committed to the well-being of society at large. If this question is not publicly debated and ways determined in which it can be honoured, it is likely that it will not happen at all. 'Environmental' accounting in a physical sense is neither a well-advanced nor an honoured art; accounting for the moral environment and general well-being is even less advanced. It would be good if we took it up.

Styles of teaching and learning strategies

In attending to the moral perspective of higher education there are implications for the way in which we treat teaching and learning. It was once said in my hearing that the only educational theory one needed to know was that *doceo*, *docere*, second conjugation, took a direct object: *I teach you*. That is not the most helpful approach. Conversely, of course, some of our seats of higher education seem to take the view that if students are incapable of learning on their own without our help, then they ought not to have been accepted on the course. Both are misleading, though if a teacher has nothing to communicate, and the student cannot learn on his or her own, then the result will be far from mutual illumination.

However, how seriously do we take the need to support our students' experience of education? The tendency to be prescriptive of certain reading, to fail to stretch our students' powers of analysis and imagination, is as much a feature of higher education as it is of the school system, leading to spoonfeeding and testing for powers of recall rather than understanding. The development of more emphasis on a student-led approach to learning will be essential with the extension of the sources on which a student will need to draw, and a growth in the range of media with which both student and tutor will, therefore, need to be familiar. But in order to facilitate this there will need to be careful attention to the support which tutors offer. Lectures are a valuable possible means of communication, but no lecturer should assume that because a lecture has occurred, communication has taken place. Indeed, our faith in lectures is touching, but not necessarily helpful. We would do better to look to them for the encouragement of enthusiasm to study, so that students will want to get on with their own thinking, reading and experiment, or opportunities to develop themes which are otherwise unobtainable or not readily extractable from the literature. And then it will mean that it is the response of the tutor to the student's work, on paper and in seminar or tutorial, which will be fundamental to the learning process.

For this interaction to be effective, the return of work with a bare mark on it is all but valueless. What the student can do to improve his work should be stated, errors of judgement or argument indicated and discussed, and further suggestions for reading made. Our capacity to teach is impaired, of course, by the low value which the institution gives to the role of the teacher: and yet as institutions what are we doing if we are not seen to be celebrating and encouraging the art of enabling our students to learn? It is fundamental that we take it seriously.

Assessment is an area to which special attention should also be given. The school system has been reviewed and with much heart-searching and no lack of controversy, a new pattern of assessment has been introduced. It will be important that we do the same. The supposition that continuous assessment, combined with an element of examination, seen or unseen, somehow sums up what we are about and enables us to produce the judgements we should want to produce on student performance seems inadequate. Assessment must enable us to know where a student is, help us to recognize what we have successfully taught, and provide clues for both as to what might be the next best way to take matters forward. But what are we assessing? Not simply powers of recall, we also want to test understanding, powers of application, critical acumen, judgement. But even these are limited. Could we devise an element of assessment which involved group work, which involved creativity, which tested the capacity to respond to pressure quickly and on one's feet, to be persuasive? Are these matters 'non-academic' in the sense that they do not refer to the student's performance on a given course of study? If we hold that view then we should look to the wider purposes for which higher education exists, and which, therefore, we should be taking into account when assessing the performance of our students, and the design and significance of our courses. As responsible persons, our graduates will be working in teams, having to think quickly and express themselves accurately and cogently under stress, and having to be persuasive as well as knowledgeable. Are these not matters which we can attend to with profit when we discuss styles of teaching and learning strategies? Does our moral purpose not assume that we will?

Research and staff development

It is difficult to see how one can teach if one is not learning. But there are some distinctions to be made here. To rely on last year's notes, or – even worse – one's last year's memory, as if that would always be an adequate basis for passing on knowledge, is to mistake what human knowledge is. And so the assimilation of books, the reading of articles, the pursuit of matters of concern will be crucial to one's ability to introduce and develop a student's ability to participate in a specific universe of discourse. But equally, it is vital that one should have to hold one's own with one's peers, that critical discussion, perhaps publication, certainly the giving of papers, should be an assumed necessity for the development and maintenance of the capacity to teach effectively.

Research might be thought to be another matter especially if it is defined as adding to the sum total of human knowledge. The expansion of higher education which has taken place, and more particularly the expansion which is likely to take place, simply makes it unlikely that all those who are legitimately involved in the teaching and who fulfil their responsibilities utterly in that regard, are themselves all capable of adding anything worth having to the sum total of human knowledge. It seems best, therefore, not to assume it, and not to presume what in principle is undeliverable. On the other hand, an institution of higher education which is not committed as a community to research will be defective. The limit of what we know must be apparent, the means and opportunities of enquiry must be understood, the value of research shared, even if it is only some members of a department, a faculty or an institution who are actually engaged in it. Scholarship is for all; research for those who are most adept. Of course, a proper celebration of the role of teaching and the art of the teacher will help to put right the very serious disparity of esteem which is affecting our judgement in this area.

But all this has implications for staff development. The distribution of resources by the institution will be a judgement on its moral perspective. So the identification and support of ways in which teaching can be improved, will be as important as the development of research in the life of an academic community. Something significant is done by the support of scholarship, by financing attendance at conferences; but attention to teaching styles and learning strategies through courses, discussion, visiting lecturers, schools to provide familiarity with information technology, may all be as important. And also a review and discussion of styles and patterns of assessment will be required with the expectation that many colleagues will need to have even some of the basics explained. In the last resort, but very importantly, it would also be interesting if even the art of writing references was examined. What do we need to know, for what purpose, and how can it best be said with honesty and clarity for the benefit of the employer and prospective employee?

Pattern, range and purpose in higher education: a collaborative model

The pattern of higher education is quite clear in most minds: it is a three-year programme of intensive study (longer, of course, if you are intending to be a doctor) leading to a first degree, which may or may not lead to further study. It is full-time, free, but a privilege not to be expected for the vast majority of the population for whom it would be inappropriate. While there has been much discussion of other possible patterns, and some modest progress in respect of part-time credit accumulation and credit transfer, this for the most part closely approximates to the truth.

It is not a situation which is helpful if the wide needs of the community are to be met, and therefore it is not one which is in the best interests of the institutions. It is vital that we at least double the number of students in higher education, that we have a much more flexible approach to the length, assessment and organization of programmes of work and that we look at the funding involved in order to make it possible. While this is no doubt a matter on which there would now be little disagreement, in principle, there would be much to debate with regard to implementation. But the point to be emphasized here is the moral one. If what we have to offer is of value to individuals and through them to the community, then we have a duty to organize ourselves in such a way as to be able to offer it to the widest cross-section and the largest proportion of those who could directly benefit. And this is all the more a matter of concern if the purposes of our institutions are to educate in the widest sense and not simply to be the agents for the distribution of knowledge and skills. And in order to retain our integrity the diversification and extension of the patterns in which higher education is offered will raise with greater sharpness the question of how we fulfil the responsibility to the community for the quality of the person as well as his or her academic performance.

The range of courses and institutions is also a matter of some interest, for it is by no means clear that what should be included in higher education has not been too rigidly defined, and the range of styles and types of institution tending to reduce and so limit scope for interesting those who should be our students. On the first count one would mention nursing and on the second the management initiatives, rather than the educational or the moral perspective, which have tended to reduce student choice and to cultivate a climate of uniformity rather than diversity. Diversity of management, of course profile, of provenance, and identity of the specific traditions which one cultivates, must all be welcomed as ingredients of a system which is to maintain the possibility of growth and adaptation in relation to the demands of society while at the same time remaining clear about the role which it plays itself.

The model inherent in this thesis is that of collaboration. None of us is large enough now to meet the diversity of demands which society puts upon us: all of us need to look to one another in collaboration to be able to meet even a proportion of them. This need for collaboration is not a function of size so it is more a matter of the range of interactions open to a set of institutions, each with its own expertise, history and purposes, as opposed to that which is open to a single institution whatever its size. A commitment to develop breadth of range in institutional character will itself change the depth of interaction between higher education, the schools, industry, and the society at large. The latter is particularly important since too great a proportion of our society regards higher education as privileged, private, isolationist and of dubious value. For all that things are changing, it requires decisive action to maintain and increase the momentum.

And the collaborative mode must distinguish not only our sense of inter-dependence as institutions in a common system, but our willingness to collaborate with industry and the private market as well as government and the public domain. It is not simply that the climate of political discussion has changed, which it has, and that, therefore, if the resources are to be available to enable students and institutions to provide for their needs and contribute to the public good, the marketplace is where we shall have to go, it is also that this interaction is capable potentially of bringing benefits to both. The snag comes if institutions of higher education ape the styles and seek merely to embody the values of the market. In any collaboration one expects there to be distinct and identifiable contributions from each party. When that happens, continued collaboration and further mutual exploration of interests is likely to take place. If, on the other hand, one partner simply offers services, it will always be worth the other's considering whether it would not be more cost-effective, and offer easier parameters for management, if it provided the services itself.

But as academic communities, our institutions of higher education offer more than mere services. Our commitment to intellectual enquiry for its own sake, the respect for academic freedom, the wholeness of our perspectives notwithstanding the particularity of our specialisms, the attention to the quality of the product, the person of the graduate, all combine to offer a basis for the confidence with which we can contribute to collaborative ventures. There is no attempt to be complete in stating these morally desirable qualities of higher education, neither is there any claim for exclusivity as if higher education alone recommended them; but it is crucial to say that without them higher education is not worthy of the name.

Conclusion

A society which creates a higher education system through which graduates are not encouraged to gain knowledge of themselves and to take responsibility for their knowledge and skills, will soon discover that it lacks the resources to take the whole community into account when making decisions, and in particular when considering matters which affect the long-term future. Apart from the acquisition of a language in which moral issues can be seen to be significant, how will we discuss cogently matters which are beyond the immediate concerns of our present experience? What reason could we possibly have for extending it? But a higher education system is concerned with the quality of the society in which we live, it is concerned with fundamental questions of human well-being, it is concerned to create 'an educated community'; as such it must look at the moral perspective which it presents. Society must also look to the moral purpose as well as the vital practical importance of higher education. The two are, of course, not mutually exclusive, but if the former is not emphasized, the latter will lack vision and ultimately coherence.

Notes

1 Karl Jaspers, quoted by John Farquharson, in review printed in the *Times Higher Educational Supplement*, 20 January 1989, p. 19.
2 Derek Bok, *Beyond the Ivory Tower*, Harvard University Press, 1982, p. 73.
3 Alan B. Cobban, *The Mediaeval English Universities*, Scolar Press, 1988, p. 173, 347.

4 J. H. Newman, *The Idea of a University*, ed. I. T. Ker, Clarendon Press, O.U.P. 1976, p. v.
5 Ibid., pp. 154–5.
6 Quoted in Howard H. Peckham, *The Making of the University of Michigan*, University of Michigan Press, 1967, p. 34. It is interesting that Newman should have delivered his Discourses to audiences in Dublin in 1852, the year after Tappan published his reflections on university education in the United States.
7 J. H. Newman, *The Idea of a University*, p. 154.
8 Lord Chancellor's Office, *Committee on the Age of Majority Report*, HMSO, 1967.

5

Academics and Society:
Freedom's Seamless Robe

Christopher Price

'Academic freedom' has been used in different contexts with different meanings and for different purposes. At one end of the spectrum it is used as an ideological and sectarian slogan and employed by academics in defence of their privileges and against institutions they dislike – whether these be political parties, governments, university paymasters or university administrations and hier-archies. At the other it is an expression of the fundamental aspiration – and some might say duty – of the teacher and researcher in a university to pursue truth wherever the quest may lead. In between, it is used imprecisely as shorthand to describe the current apprehensions of academics in the face of university reform. Sometimes attempts are made to limit the cadre of academic teachers to whom the concept – or the privilege – should properly apply.

This paper starts by analysing the political background to the use of the word 'freedom' in an educational context. It then goes on to assert that academic freedom, as defined at the non-ideological end of the spectrum, is an essential part of the mission of any higher education institution, an aspiration which can never *belong* to academics (or indeed to anyone else) by right but must always be *claimed* by them, sometimes with difficulty and always with moral courage, and an aspiration which can never be special to academics, much less to a particular class of academics, but is akin to similar aspirations and duties properly claimed by all those involved in the transmission of information, knowledge and values in society. Finally, the paper discusses how far recent 'industrial' involvement in higher education represents a threat to academic freedom.

Academic freedom as political and ideological rhetoric

For over two decades now, the debate about academic freedom has taken place in an atmosphere of a struggle between proponents of 'Left' and 'Right' ideology in which both are prone to try to appropriate the word 'freedom' to themselves. This is particularly true in an era when both universities in particular and higher education in general are subject to pressure and change driven by external forces – declining demographic supply, rapidly escalating technology and changing employer demand for graduates, political and social demands for greater access by and equity towards the taxpaying population at large, and ever more stringent budgets. In particular, the place of universities in society and the perception of the economic realities of higher education have changed a great deal since the late 1960s when a public debate last took place on the concept of academic freedom.

Then the rhetoric of 'freedom' in higher education was firmly in the grip of the Left. (Indeed, that was one of the reasons why the Black Paper authors felt urged to publish their tracts.) The Council for Academic Freedom and Democracy[1] was founded partly as an attempt to consolidate the advances in autonomy some academics had experienced over the late 1960s and partly in an attempt to combat the revisionist phenomenon of 'Warwick University Ltd'[2] – a new university overtly prioritizing its links with industry and 'industrial values' over its commitment to internal democracy and its duties to society. The label pinned on this latter phenomenon, intended as pejorative in 1972, today describes the values the government would wish universities to embrace.

From the Right, the idea of educational freedom was also being discussed in the Black Papers – but in two contradictory senses. In *Black Paper Two*, both (the then) Max Beloff and D. C. Watt of the London School of Economics criticized the universities for undue subservience not only to egalitarian fashion but also to the new *dirigisme* of the University Grants Committee (UGC), prophesying that both these phenomena would result in a loss of 'academic freedom'.[3] Academic freedom was equated to an assumption that the agenda of higher education should be firmly in the grip of academics who thought as they did.

Freedom, however, in other parts of the educational habitat, turned out to be something of a dirty word, connoting 'free' teaching methods and encapsulating everything the authors wanted to get rid of; also in *Black Paper Two*, Sir Cyril Burt (just before his research methods were exposed as hopelessly flawed and his academic credibility finally destroyed), in an article asserting a long decline in educational standards over the previous 50 years, declares:

> Parents and members of the public are beginning to wonder whether the free discipline, or lack of discipline, in the new permissive school may not largely be responsible for much of the delinquency, violence and general unrest that characterise our permissive society.[4]

Antitheses of 'freedom' like discipline, order and traditional values of the old regime formed the authors' agenda. Throughout the Black Papers 'freedom for universities from interference by government' was a *desideratum*. 'Freedom for teachers and pupils from traditional curricular restraints' was to be deplored. It was assumed throughout that greater 'arm's length' autonomy should prevail for the UGC to protect universities but no such system was necessary to protect academic freedom in colleges and schools; and that though the taxpayer, like the piper, should have the right generally to call the tune, the universities should be an exception to this rule.

Of all the Black Paper authors, only Max Beloff faced this problem honestly by founding the independent University in Buckingham to be free of all UGC control and taxpayers' money – apart from student grants, which he felt able to accept as soon as the privilege was granted to him. Some thought this might start a trend of other similar independent universities; in fact it did not – though the creeping privatization of all universities and polytechnics may eventually have much the same effect, if the free market model of Mr Robert Jackson MP, the present Parliamentary Secretary at the Department of Education and Science, prevails over the Treasury's insistence on control by manpower planning.

This discontinuity on the Right about freedom in education persists; and both their authoritarian and libertarian pedigrees are still discernible. Compulsory testing in state schools and a compulsory national curriculum seem to come easily from a government which still speaks the rhetoric of freedom. In reality, legislation for 'freedom' is becoming a crude device to implant values in the curriculum which are acceptable to the government and to exclude those associated with local education authorities or teachers themselves. Compulsion is quietly introduced into 'value' areas of the school system (physics, history, religious education) while freedom is loudly proclaimed in an economic context. These exercises have nothing to do with freedom – they are part of an attempt to reduce public expenditure, to sharpen up the hidden curriculum of competition within educational institutions by creating overt competition between them, and to transfer the ownership, in both secondary and higher education, of the power to transmit knowledge, information and values from the teachers and the students to government, employers and parents.

This increased use of the concept of academic freedom for political ends has sprung partly from the 'liberal' rhetoric of the Institute of Economic Affairs – which is now a compulsory starting point for the development of all government social policy and threatens to become a new consensus accepted by all, even the great and the good of the old regime. Thus, paradoxically, side by side with authoritarian policies, the concepts of 'freedom' in education are being appropriated by the rhetoric of the Right.

This is, of course, part of a general shift in the political climate. It has also come about through a determined effort by commentators on the Right to change political perceptions of freedom and oppression. Caroline Cox first described her experiences with left-wing students as a polytechnic lecturer in *Rape of Reason*.[5] Since then she and her various collaborators have created, with generous assistance from elements of the national (if not the educational) press, a new demonology of 'oppressors'. These no longer include Max Beloff's UGC or indeed any element of central government (the butt and bogeyman of educational 'freedom' protesters for 150 years) but rather Marxist-dominated students' unions and far Left Labour-controlled local education authorities in London.[6] The attack has been pursued for a decade now by much of the popular press of the Right and in particular by Paul Johnson, in the *Daily Mail*, who first began to use the epithet 'fascist' to describe protest by the Left.

Side by side with these 'oppressor' demons, there has been presented an angelic company of honest 'victims' – in particular, teachers and lecturers fighting to be allowed to teach *their* curriculum with *their* methods. As a result the

Black Paper *epigoni*[7] have now succeeded, under the Thatcher government, in going very much further than their pamphleteer predecessors and becoming an alternative educational civil service, beloved of Downing Street and snapping at the heels of the Department of Education and Science and education ministers, who are often perceived to be moving too slowly in the implementation of proposed authoritarian educational measures, whether in re-establishing a traditional curriculum or in ridding the schools of left-wing influence generally. Their most coveted prize has been the final elimination of the Inner London Education Authority in the Education Reform Act 1988. The only two achievements of the 1960s and 1970s to have withstood the tide so far are the comprehensive principle (in so far as the 11-plus examination has not been overtly brought back) and the General Certificate of Secondary Education examination, finally sanctioned by Sir Keith Joseph after being hatched, over a 14-year incubation period, by some of the 'old Left' curricular freedom campaigners.[8]

Legislation on issues of 'freedom' in higher education has also followed the commentators of the Right. 'Freedom of speech' legislation, successfully introduced by Caroline Cox in the House of Lords against the government's wishes, was originally aimed at students' unions – to force them to abandon 'no platform' policies and grant hearings to South African and other (sometimes allegedly racist) speakers. But its effect was to force 'Left liberal' institutions to give a platform to 'authoritarian Right' ideas – and incidentally to make the *management* of institutions that much more difficult. One cannot escape the impression that higher education was being targeted for freedom of speech legislation not because of any genuine concern about academic freedom in universities but to expose their liberal culture to political confrontation. They are currently seen by government as *dangerously* free and obstinately impervious to the New Right ideology. While the government preaches academic freedom it behaves like Cromwell in occupation of Magdalen College, Oxford.

In another piece of legislative action, the government insists it has given the polytechnics the 'freedom' to manage their own affairs – on the basis of legislation to 'liberate' them from local councils. But ironically, the legislation imposes a managerial pattern which makes it possible, if the managers should so wish, to override genuine academic freedom – the right of lecturers to teach their own presentation of the curriculum in their own way at their own pace. In neither of these cases do the rhetoric of freedom and the reality of the outcome mesh.

Control over the transmission of information and values has certainly been treated more favourably in higher education than elsewhere. Other institutions whose traditional, constitutional role has been in the past to guard against totalitarianism and play a critical role in society are being curbed rather than freed. Contrary to a strong previous principle of common law, the new Official Secrets Act will put editors, journalists and civil servants who disturb the political tranquility by exposing iniquity in high places at risk of prosecution under the criminal law and imprisonment for two years. A national curriculum will shackle teachers in state schools – especially those of the Jean Brodie type who believe in personal and idiosyncratic approaches to the curriculum and teaching methods. Local government is subject to new, draconian legislation about what information local officials and councillors may legally purvey – legislation of a kind which central government would not dream of imposing on itself. Trade unions, though still at liberty to put forward a point of view, are subject to more stringent curbs over the use of their funds than ever before. In the media, where the increasing concentration of private oligopolistic ownership itself limits freedom, there are also new statutory curbs on television and radio (the ban on IRA interviews and new interventionist regulatory councils), while there is no sympathy in government with the idea of similar freedom for the citizen in the form of 'right of reply' legislation.

Education, in its literature and philosophy through the ages, has always been associated with the 'freedom' and liberation of the human spirit in a way which has never been associated with any political ideology. Until 1968 and the Black Papers, though there was always controversy about education, a certain consensus existed on this basis. In nineteenth-century England, Edward Thring of Uppingham and Sidney Webb of the London County Council both spoke the same 'liberal' language on education. The debate over the past two decades, however, has not addressed itself to the core of this connection between education, on the one side, and freedom, on the other. Since the Black Paper authors helped destroy the educational consensus[9] 20 years ago, much of the educational rhetoric of the Right has been co-opted into a political struggle to gain control of the transmission of information, values and culture in society. From that point of view it has had little in common with genuine arguments about academic freedom.

Academic freedom and courage

True academic freedom concerns not some objective 'freedom' to be bestowed, at the behest of the state, upon a selected cadre of individuals but upon the personal integrity of teachers in universities and polytechnics. In Eastern Europe, it is the universities which have succeeded in containing and protecting men and women of integrity in the pre-Gorbachev era. When Greece was under a fascist dictatorship 20 years ago, it was among the teachers and students of the polytechnic that the revolt against the junta took place. Neither the universities nor the individuals concerned were ever 'granted' academic freedom by the authorities. Academics took it for themselves, always in circumstances of difficulty and intimidation. One current fear in UK universities and polytechnics is that under the new influences of government *diktat*, industrial paymasters and privatization, academics will be frightened to teach in the way they think best and speak out when they think it right. The only ultimate answer is simply not to be frightened or intimidated.

In this sense, the government is wanting to have its cake and eat it on academic freedom. It hopes to privatize the universities and polytechnics in terms of their financial framework but keep them nationalized in terms of their corporate duty to the nation. It will be important not to allow the economic fear which privatization is calculated to induce to spill over among academic teachers into a lack of belief in themselves and in the values their institutions were founded to disseminate. If we think it right to teach sociology in a particular way, we should teach it so; if heads of institutions do not like what the government (or anyone else) is doing, they should say so; their words should put courage into their professors. We should emulate the honourable tradition in Eastern Europe of the academic community being in the front line against the erosion of democracy and the power of authoritarian government. We in the United Kingdom should be no less courageous than academics in Czechoslovakia or Poland.

This will not come easily since courage has in the United Kingdom not been a necessary academic virtue of late. The links between university and state have been at best harmonious and at worst too close for comfort. The relationship served us well in the Second World War when Oxbridge brainpower was recruited to win the war; it has served us less well more recently as big government – from the Ministry of Defence to the Research Councils and the DES itself – have been allowed to acquire an unhealthily large slice of university scientific and technological research. It could well be a required quality for the future.

The seamless robe of freedom

Nor will university academics be alone in needing this courage. In the development of literature, journalism and the trade unions, freedom has never been something to be received from above. It is something brave people take, knowing the risks, planning and working together and driven by a determination to hold fast to values in which they believe. Until teachers in universities and polytechnics begin to discuss academic freedom in these terms, it is easy to imagine them sliding over the next decade into being a comparatively well-funded, complaisant new 'estate of the realm', enjoying their privileges but neither inspiring the rising generation with free and democratic values nor truly pushing back the frontiers of knowledge. Those free and democratic values need an atmosphere of academic freedom in which to flourish.

The most successful of the big corporations – IBM, ICI and Shell – know only too well that simply hiring clever graduates is not enough. They want to steer the knowledge, abilities and skills which they pay for in a coherent direction for the benefit of the company. Many universities would insist that they are different; they do not want to do this; they want to bring together 'free spirits' who could never break the frontiers of knowledge and understanding if they were forced into such a narrow straightjacket. To some, therefore, academic freedom involves particular privileges and a particular role for a tiny elite to which society may be willing to entrust this 'free-roving' mission.

I do not believe there is any longer any political or social consensus for this primitive idea of a protected intellectual 'playpen' for a minority of academics.

If academics are to receive publicly supported salaries (as opposed to privately supported ones at Buckingham) they will increasingly have a duty to work within some social and institutional mission. Indeed mission statements are already being required of all institutions within the Polytechnics and Colleges Funding Council (PCFC) sector and they will soon be demanded of universities by the UFC. These mission statements need not and should not erode academic freedom by interfering with deeply held belief. But they will require academics to work together rather more. The lonely, publicly supported, academic is becoming an animal of the past; the corporate higher education institution arrived some time ago in the United States and has now come to the United Kingdom. It will involve new senses of direction and will entail institutions becoming clearer about objectives.

If this is the direction in which higher education is going, constitutional change will be necessary, especially in the universities. The great reforms of the late 1960s, when students were first allowed into the decision-making process, were necessary. But these reforms have now run themselves out; they no longer give the institution any drive or impact. It is now necessary for the first time for universities to negotiate their place in society at large. In that negotiation, any elitist formulation of academic freedom will be profoundly unhelpful, whether to the universities, the government or to the rest of society. What our society needs is a framework within which to give a far wider range of people a taste of academic freedom – not just at the age of 18 but at all stages of adult life. The academic community – and the academic elite within it to which I return later – must enlist a far larger constituency to help redefine academic freedom.

Elites versus the new managerial climate

How much will the abolition of tenure and the imposition of funding bodies equipped with quite new interventionist powers erode academic freedom? What will be the effect of the new 'managerial' atmosphere in higher education, foreshadowed in Kenneth Baker's speech at Lancaster in January 1989 (when he opted for a US university model in the United Kingdom)[10] and currently encouraged by increasing financial stringency in university budgets?

The argument as the Education Reform Bill was going through the House of Lords did produce a useful form of words (passed against the wishes of the government) which has now been entrenched in legislation[11] for the universities and into Articles of Government for the polytechnics and colleges. Though many lawyers say it has little legal effect, it will be some safeguard against the worst excesses of any future McCarthyite witchhunt in UK higher education.

On tenure, a distinction has to be made between its formality and its reality. Certainly, its abolition in universities is in the spirit of the Thatcherite age; and in the immediate aftermath of its abolition, a certain twitchiness may develop among some academics, perhaps causing some of them to worry rather than work; but not, I suspect, among the best or even the average ones. Polytechnics in England and Wales have never had formal tenure and universities overseas have tended to limit the privilege to a quite small number of academics. The row over tenure, I suspect, will quickly die.

The row over the powers of the Universities Funding Council (UFC) and the PCFC, however, may continue for rather longer. The recent Education Reform Act found the government cleanly split. The dry Right wanted to privatize the universities, thus encouraging more competition among them (and between them and the polytechnics) and reducing government intervention to a minimum; they were even happy to contemplate a single funding body on these grounds. The wet Left were much keener on maintaining the binary system and with it an Athenaeum-based 'secret garden' for the universities, partly to resist the challenge of the cheaper polytechnics but also to try to preserve an elite version of academic freedom. A separate UFC, they felt, might better preserve academic freedom and leave the PCFC to be more *dirigiste* with the polytechnics. The UFC has been slow to get off the ground. It is not at all clear yet how far this stratagem has succeeded.

Corporate policies imply institutional management – a concept wholly alien to the culture of the English and Welsh university. There is little doubt that one aspect of university academic freedom in the past was the fact that academics would not demean to be 'managed' or even appraised. They liked to feel they were different and to some of them that was what academic freedom was all about. The idle have been allowed to be idle. The curious to be curious. The cloister, some feel, should be an asylum of peace to those (like Laurie Taylor's Dr Piercemuller in his *Times Higher Education Supplement* column) who prefer it that way. It should also, of course, be a creative and peaceful workshop for the energetic and industrious. This has always been the basis of the classic argument for academic freedom for an elite and that elite alone. Mere polytechnic lecturers should be managed; true university academics should not.

The advocates of this elite concept of academic freedom tend to produce a priori arguments and rely less on history or international comparisons. Research and scholarship in the United States does not seem to have suffered from a tougher management regime. Many US universities, though managerially run, seem able to recruit staff more successfully than UK ones. In good universities and polytechnics genuine scholars usually get on with their scholarship. There is no evidence that the presence or absence of tenure or tough management affects the willingness of academics to teach and write freely.

The elite argument centres round one of three types of academic freedom set out in a recent *THES* editorial.[12] It is an analogue to clinical freedom in the medical profession, according to which none but a small circle of academic colleagues can ever be competent to teach and research in a particular field.[13] According to this argument, true university education should be sharply distinguished from other forms of higher education; only a small number of the elect can be admitted to it. The test for admission is an ability to understand and wish to explore a particular subject in depth. It is a reactionary trend in the literal meaning of the word – it looks back for examples to boost its case. Its gods are, after Plato, Cardinal Newman and F. R. Leavis. The principal figure in its modern demonology is Lord Robbins, who is (wrongly) credited with having expanded higher education and stimulating the student revolt in the 1960s. One of its latest exponents is Professor Anthony O'Hear of Bradford University, who has contributed to at least one chapter in a book on academic freedom[14] and newspaper articles on the unsuitability of the General Certificate of Secondary Education as a preparation for A level and university.[15] In 'Academic Freedom and the University', he goes for Plato without the Republic – asserting a purported privilege for an intellectual elite to be supported by the state to seek and contemplate truth in certain university surroundings, without any further corresponding implied platonic duty that they should contribute in any specific or direct way to the running of the democracy.

It is an old-fashioned idea which may be about to become fashionable again. It was at the heart of the old 11-plus and the ultra-restrictive system of university entrance which followed it. It was an idea which held sway in England and Wales for a period before and after the Second World War when the classically educated mandarins like Sir Cyril Norwood enlisted the new psychometrists like Sir Cyril Burt (knighthoods abounded for educationalists in those days) to produce a scientific justification for a platonic set of classes in society.[16] In practical terms, that scheme failed because it proved impossible to pick the high flyers with any real precision; and it was judged unfair that school organization should be distorted by such selection as such a high priority; and that the school curriculum should be irrelevant to all those who were not going to enter the elite. It is also impossible to guarantee that the chosen elite universities will remain worthy of such privilege. All too soon the ivory towers in which you put the academic elect sink into the sort of sloth which Gibbon discovered in the monks of Magdalen. The government is currently floating plans to select a few very well-funded, 'research' universities; but there is no suggestion that the elite characteristic of such universities should extend to their selection of under-graduates.

I suspect that the nostalgia for the idea of limited academic freedom for a small elite will be overtaken by a mixture of new technology and competition in higher education. The Thatcher government is clearly on course to erode maintenance grants and further *privatize* higher education – which will further tip the balance in giving rich young people a decided edge over clever young people in admission to universities. Universities want clever youngsters, not just rich ones. Yet Chaucer's 'poor scholar of Oxenford' is already making way for yuppie offspring, in search of an access course to the City rather than an academic experience. The intellectual elect wandering untroubled through the groves of academe may be a beautiful, nostalgic idea. But it is against the spirit of a practical, thrusting competitive age.

It also runs clean against the nature of modern knowledge. We are in the age of the polymath not the mathematician, the interdisciplinary team rather than the master of the discipline; in one academic 'field' after another discrete boundaries crumble. Chemical engineers and biologists must pool their wisdom to become biotechnologists, economists are lost without political scientists, the old divisions between electrical and mechanical engineering become increasingly meaningless as both depend on design, computing systems and business sense. Knowledge and enquiry no longer go on in the ancient, discrete subjects. Something very much more flexible than the old university model is necessary if we are to cope and make connections in both natural and social science.

More threatening still, academics are losing what monopoly position they once had. New groves of academe are springing up outside the university system. The received wisdom of medicine, the law and science are increasingly under attack from consumer and environmentalist 'lay' opinion. 'Natural medicine' and new therapies flourish. The omniscient academic priesthood finds it more and more difficult to survive, not just because the single subject becomes an interdisciplinary spectrum but also because some academic fields are put off the academic agenda altogether. 'Consultants' from firms which once contented themselves with adding up accounts, now profess to train folk and investigate subjects in a fraction of the time which universities and polytechnics have traditionally taken. The river is moving too fast to preserve the traditional university academy intact. If universities really want to continue to occupy the intellectual high ground in future, they will have to work for it, earn it and struggle each year to hold it. Such a scenario does not fit either with the historical separation of universities from polytechnics or with any arbitrary selection by government of a group of elite research universities.

The new intruders – the industrial connection and the mature clientele

One of David Lodge's most popular novels, *Nice Work*, described the culture shock of a middle-aged male Birmingham managing director changing places with a younger female Birmingham University lecturer. Something of the same process is happening in higher education – particularly in polytechnics at the moment – as new bemused industrial governors peek inside the institution and discover what is really going on. There is sometimes a feeling of folk from different planets, staring across an abyss at each other. Government ministers are keen on the idea and seem to believe that this process will produce a sort of industrial magic and that contact with industrialists will transform our institutions overnight.

Some universities and polytechnics have had close relations with industrialists for years. Indeed, many of the nineteenth-century redbrick universities were founded in close association with industry. The change is that in polytechnics a new group of industrialists are taking, for the first time, a direct role in the management of the institution. I have yet to see any evidence that this process is threatening academic freedom. True, our new governors are less patient of delay – they expect decisions to be taken quickly. There will be an urgency, a quickening of pace in some places which could possibly disturb the traditional, leisurely civilized atmosphere. But there is no industrial predisposition to interfere in academic decisions. I personally find the new industrial connection a breath of fresh air.

In reality, however, the industrial connection is just one of a number of new pressures on the traditional academic; and, I suspect, more profound changes will follow in the wake of technology and greater understanding of the way in which students learn. Universities and polytechnics must be helped to break out of the routine of decanting out-of-date knowledge into their students – knowledge which inspired the lecturers 20 years ago but which is moving on fast all the time. The industrial connection may help us to widen our clientele; but it will only be worthwhile if it impacts on the whole institution and widens both our clientele and our curriculum.

For the second culture shock which universities face over the next decade will be the advent of the mature student – in more than penny numbers. The values that these students bring with them will help breathe new life into both the learning process and what is learnt. We shall see more part-time students, more distance learning, more modular courses and a general shift to accommodate the needs of the student/customer. Some of the changes may be denounced as a threat to academic freedom. I do not think that any of them will be. But neither industrialist nor mature student will tolerate the concept of an intellectual elite which defines academic freedom in such a way as to exclude them from the secret groves.

I believe that it is government rather than industry that will prove to be the real enemy of academic freedom. The proof of the pudding will be the state of higher education at the end of the decade. Governments the world over are becoming more centralist, the United Kingdom's no less than any other. They are becoming daily more sophisticated in the control and management of information. They will therefore always be suspicious of the institutions which form young minds. They want to own and orchestrate the universities just as their friends now own and orchestrate the media. It is not in the government's ultimate interest to see a lively, critical and free new generation to emerge from university each year. It would prefer a more vocationally trained[17] and programmed workforce. Preventing outside forces from achieving this particular objective is what academic freedom is all about. At the end of the day the freedom of the true academic is no different from that of each and every citizen who is committed to the maintenance of democratic values and to restraints on a totalitarian society.

Notes

1 The word 'democracy' seems to have been added at the last minute in prophetic anticipation of the later colonization of the phrase by the Right.

2 E. P. Thompson (ed.), *Warwick University Ltd: Industry, Management and the Universities*, Penguin Education Special, 1970.

3 Max Beloff, 'Oxford: A Lost Cause' and D. C. Watt, 'The Freedom of the Universities: Illusion and Reality, 1962–9' both in C. B. Cox and A. E. Dyson (eds), *Black Paper Two: The Crisis in Education*, Critical Quarterly Society, 1969. The fact that the (Labour) governments *dirigisme* of 1968 would be quite minuscule compared with the substantial constitutional control imposed by its political opponents 20 years later through the Education Reform Act 1988 could not of course have been prophesied at the time.

4 Sir Cyril Burt, 'The Mental Differences between Children' in Cox and Dyson, *Black Paper Two*, p. 24.

5 Keith Jacka, Caroline Cox and John Marks, *Rape of Reason*, Churchill Press, 1976.

6 In fact the coupling of the left-wing interventionist policies of the Inner London Education Authority with the problems of one polytechnic was somewhat unreasonable. For well over a decade the principal charge against ILEA in relation to its polytechnics was one of failure to impose accountability and of chronic *laissez-faire* neglect.

7 I use this word advisedly. The *Shorter Oxford English Dictionary* defines it as 'One of a succeeding (and less distinguished) generation.'

8 Now that it is under attack from the Left for being expensive, bureaucratic and redundant, and from the Right as too egalitarian, it could be squeezed out of existence by both.

9 C. B. Cox and A. E. Dyson, 'Letter to Members of Parliament' in Cox and Dyson, *Black Paper Two*, p. 15.

10 'Baker's Vision for the Next 25 Years', *Times Higher Education Supplement*, 13 January 1989, p. 7.

11 The Education Reform Bill, Section 202(2), says:

> In regard to these functions the [University] Commissioners shall have regard to the need –
> (a) to ensure that academic staff have freedom within the law to question and test received wisdom, and to put forward new ideas and controversial or unpopular opinions, without placing themselves in jeopardy of losing their jobs or privileges they may have at their institutions.

12 *THES*, 30 December 1988.

13 The two other examples of academic freedom were: a freedom to say 'outrageous' things in challenging received wisdom; and a freedom to do 'outrageous' things in practice, by subverting existing institutions. The second is now protected in law and the third is most commonly practised in our redbrick universities by professional senators. University College, Cardiff, came to grief partly through elements of this variety of spurious academic freedom.

14 A. O'Hear, 'Academic Freedom and the University' in M. Tight (ed.), *Academic Freedom and Responsibility*, SRHE/Open University Press, 1988.

15 Cf. A. O'Hear, 'Failing the Test', Yorkshire Post, 17 December 1988. Preparation for university entrance was never intended as a primary purpose of GCSE.

16 It is true that Sir Cyril Burt, 'The organization of schools', in C. B. Cox and A. E. Dyson (eds), *Black Paper Three: Goodbye Mr Short*, Critical Quarterly Society, 1970, p. 17, insists that he rejected the Norwood typology of children who might fit the new grammar, technical and modern schools as 'a theory as out of date as phrenology'. But he did insist in the Appendix to the Hadow Report of 1931 that primary schools should be streamed and secondary schools differentiated by type. Norwood and Burt share paternal responsibility for the old 11-plus.

17 I do not imply from this that I favour 'academic' over 'vocational' courses in higher education. Many so called 'academic' courses prepare for a well-paid vocation in any case. I simply advocate the injection of values into all courses, whatever their 'level' or label.

6

A Consensus Framework for Higher Education

Peter Slee

My hopes for higher education in the 1990s depend upon removing the blind spot that has halted its progress in the 1980s. The last decade has been a disaster for higher education in the United Kingdom. Resources have been depleted, morale shattered, all sense of clear purpose and direction abandoned. Response to threats to higher education and doubts about its value have not prompted a spirited defence of the academic ethos by its guardians or a vision of the future by its leaders but an inward-looking, truculent trench mentality. It is at present a no-win situation, for institutions, for knowledge, for young people and for the nation.

The problem is simple enough. But to date it appears to have escaped clear diagnosis. It has *not* been the functionalization of higher education by the Right in its pursuit of solutions to economic problems. Nor has it been resistance to this by many academics in defence of their freedom, cultural purity, or sense of purpose. No, the crisis in higher education, though revolving around two divergent sets of views, is not defined by them, but rather by the marked unwillingness of those conducting the debate to admit to a consensus framework into which distinct but equally valid objectives for higher education can fit, and then to develop a formula by which they can peacefully coexist.

If higher education is to play a full and positive role in the United Kingdom in the 1990s, those involved in shaping policy and national and institutional levels must take three fundamental steps. First, there must be a clear recognition on all sides that higher education is a multi-functional activity; and that it addresses three sets of needs: the need to safeguard the autonomy of knowledge; the needs of the state measured by demand for highly qualified manpower; and the needs of the individual. Balancing the demands generated by these three sets of needs has formed the unwritten sub-text of higher education in the United Kingdom for almost two hundred years. The balance has never been easy to strike. Once established, it has always been questioned, for every generation sets its own agenda for higher education in the light of changing circumstances and redefined priorities.

Second, we must recognize that because higher education is by its very nature multi-functional, then the claims made on it by these three requirements cannot be mutually exclusive but must in some sense be reconciled and dovetailed.

Third, this recognition requires open debate, compromise, planning and positive action. The chief task for higher education in the 1990s is to create and develop a framework within which the varied needs of a new generation can be met.

So what expectations for higher education are generated by its clients? And is there a fundamental incompatibility between them?

Government first. In its manifesto for higher education, the 1987 White Paper, the government makes its aspirations clear. It expects higher education to 'serve the economy more efficiently'. How? By 'achieving greater commercial and industrial relevance in higher education activity'.[1] It does not deny that higher education has other functions. But it is adamant that relevance to the world of work is paramount. And it makes it known that currently there is not enough of it in evidence.

But what of the institutions themselves? Few, I suspect, would deny that they do have a supply-side function. But precious few are prepared to rate it as a priority, and even fewer as a *raison d'être*. For most academics, 'a university is a place where scholars congregate in order thereby the better both to pursue their scholarship and to teach those who with adequate previous equipment come to enjoy the experience of participation'.[2] Against this framework, in which the autonomy of knowledge is cited as the key function of higher education, the government's White Paper appears philistine and threatening.

Jousting between government and higher education, between market philosophy and manpower planning, on the one side, and the search for truth and beauty as a good in itself, on the other, is a common theme in UK higher education. But two trends have changed the direction of higher education policy and consequently the tenor of the debate.

First, the United Kingdom is falling victim to the effects of a demographic time-bomb. It has two components. One of these is demographic decline. In 1994 nearly 25 per cent fewer 16–19-year-olds will leave school and college than did in 1988. The decline in the size of this cohort in every region in the United Kingdom will be greater than the number of 16–19-year-olds currently unemployed there. If that were not in itself sufficient cause for concern, the workforce will rise by 1.5 million over the same period. So the UK economy faces a quantitative manpower problem. As the workforce rises, the number of potential entrants to it is declining.

But that is not all. There is a second problem. The skills base is changing. The rise within the workforce will be in professional, management, craft, skilled and clerical work and will take place against a background of the steady decline of manual and unskilled labour. So while the first element of the demographic time-bomb is quantitative, the second is qualitative. The workforce of the future will need to possess on average more and higher-level skills than the workforce of today. Taken together, the two elements may have a potentially devastating effect on the UK economy. The problem faced by business is not just how to find people to do jobs, but how to find people with the potential to match the jobs' demands. In short, the United Kingdom's competitiveness and prosperity depend upon the nation's education and training systems.[3]

The second trend has had a longer lead time. And it also has two facets. In the 100 years since the state's first grant to the fledgling civic colleges in 1889, its stake in higher education has risen dramatically from £15,000 and around 6 per cent of the colleges' total expenditure, to £4.1 billion or, on average, 65 per cent of the non-research funding coming to higher education institutions today.

Additionally, this massive increase in funding has always been regarded as an investment in highly qualified manpower. And it is an investment that has always been open to review.[4] So while the Committee of Vice Chancellors and Principals stated clearly in 1947 that

> the Universities entirely accept the view that the Government has not only the right but the duty to satisfy itself . . . that the resources which are placed at the disposal of the universities are being used with full regard to both efficiency and economy,[5]

William Childs, Vice Chancellor of Reading University, had long recognized the imbalance inherent in the relationship. Academic freedom at institutional level was made possible on its present extended scale only by government funding. That alone provided the scope for institutions and individuals to determine their own mission free of 'tied money'. From the 1920s onwards, with a low number of graduates per head of population, an expanding professional, financial and state sector and labour-intensive workplace practices, both supply and demand for highly qualified manpower was evenly balanced, and easily adjusted. But Childs warned that if social and economic changes should bring in their wake new demands of a radically different order, type or scale, then, 'the universities of tomorrow may not find it easy to convince the public that they should be left alone in the enjoyment of an unorthodox autonomy'.[6]

The demographic time-bomb is just such a socio-economic shift. And it has provoked just the response Childs feared. The government is not convinced that its investment in higher education is producing the right type of highly qualified manpower to meet its economic needs. And as the major investor in the higher education system, it has begun to dictate the grounds of its continuing financial commitment. But because the pursuit of truth at the range and extent to which we have become accustomed in the United Kingdom depends so heavily on government finance, then the argument between the primacy of scholarship and the needs of the economy, whatever its moral basis, is in practical terms, uneven. The government holds the whip hand in higher education. And it now sees every reason to use it.

Nevertheless, there is a way in which the time-specific demands for the highly qualified manpower needed to defuse the demographic time-bomb, and the timeless call to the pursuit of knowledge, can both be undertaken by the same people, in the same institutions, using the same tools and the same discipline structure. The solution lies in developing within every discipline a broader framework for learning which can accommodate a range of valid educational goals.

Such a framework can be defined in two ways. First, it can be given shape by considering the needs of individuals. Second, it can be structured by clarifying the nature of the need for highly qualified manpower.

Considering the needs of individuals is highly salutary. Students have been neglected in the last ten years. But what do they expect from higher education? First and most important, they expect their learning experiences to be properly managed. And while it is this very basic requirement which gives an obvious focus for the emergence of an academic profession which conserves, disseminates and advances knowledge, few students would support the view that it was their role to act as unwitting agents for the preservation of the autonomy of knowledge. Likewise, the modern economy relies upon harnessing a significant annual cohort of highly qualified manpower. But while the aggregated behaviour of graduates as self-regarding individuals seeking to maximize their life chances may well contribute directly to the health of the economy, few students would admit to choosing their degree course with the view of improving the nation's competitiveness. In short, students cannot rightly be viewed as passive means to predetermined ends. They must be treated as ends in themselves. Education is, therefore, not an end in itself but a practical activity which should enable individuals to identify and meet their own needs. What, then, are the needs of students? They are summarized most effectively by the 1972 White Paper on higher education which stressed that

> not far from the surface of most candidates minds is the belief that higher education will go far to guarantee them a better job. All expect it to prepare them to cope more successfully with the problems that will confront them in their personal, social and working lives.[7]

In other words, higher education is expected by students to prepare them effectively for life. And for most students work will be a part of life and a large part at that. Higher education is failing students if it does not help prepare them in some way for work in the broadest sense of the word.

But what does preparation for the world of work entail? Charles Handy suggests that 'Britain's future lies in doing and making things smarter and better than our competitors'. This will be reflected in the labour market by two things. First, a rise in the general level of skills required by business, so rapid, Handy believes, that 'in 20 years time there should not be any place for unskilled workers in any organisation. Their unskilled contribution will simply not add value to pay their wages, and in consequence their work will have been largely automated, and they themselves "upskilled".'[8] Second, the application of new technology will mean that every person will have to learn to adapt his or her skills to new circumstances, or indeed, to develop new skills. Japanese engineers find that 40 per cent of their current knowledge is obsolete within four years.

The common denominator of highly qualified manpower will, therefore, be the ability to think, learn and adapt. Personal transferable skills – problem-solving, communication, teamwork – rather than technical skills defined with narrow occupational ranges, will come to form the stabilizing characteristic of work. If higher education is to meet the needs of the economy and the individual it must seek actively to develop these generic core competences that will in future define work.

But does this not undermine the multi-functional view of higher education? I think not. The processes of thought involved in problem-solving, communication and teamwork are not peculiar to any one discipline, but common to them all. Every academic discipline has, without loss of rigour, truth or substance, the potential to prepare students more effectively for the world of work.[9]

My hopes for higher education in the 1990s rest, then, only on a subtle change of emphasis and shift in organization within institutions of higher education. Academics must be prepared to act in partnership with the government that funds them and the students who are their *raison d'être*. Disciplines must be seen not as an ends in themselves but as a means to a series of ends. Process must be made as important as product. And the process which characterizes every discipline should be developed as the prime vehicle for developing the transferable intellectual skills that will come to characterize work.

In short, core competences should be identified and nurtured consciously as a legitimate aim of higher education rather than an accidental by-product of it, and it should be recognized that disciplines taught by following methodically the contours of science and scholarship, wherever they may lead, are the best means available to achieve this. The organization of knowledge should be heuristic and problem-based. Active, not passive. The apparatus of student life – the essay, seminar, tutorial, report – should not be viewed solely as a means of proving ones' industry, but *also* as a practical exercise in communication skills. Students should be encouraged to share their ideas. What in business is called co-operation, is all too often called cheating in academia. When that has been achieved then the academic discipline will be the linchpin of the multi-functional academic system.

Notes

1 Department of Education and Science, *Higher Education: Meeting the Challenge*, Cm114, HMSO, 1987 IV, 2.
2 J. Enoch Powell, 'Scholars and the State', *The Independent*, 9 March 1989, 28.
3 Institute for Employment Research, Warwick University, *Review of the Economy and Employment 1987*. For a summary, see, *Building a Stronger Partnership between Business and Secondary Education: the Report of the CBI Business Education Task Force*, CBI, 1988, pp. 25–34.
4 Peter Slee, 'Concern for Skills', *Universities Quarterly*, vol. 40, no. 2 1986, pp. 163–70.
5 Quoted by Asa Briggs, 'Development in Higher Education in the United Kingdom' in W. R. Niblett (ed.), *Higher Education, Demand and Response*, Tavistock, 1969, 100–1.
6 W. M. Childs, 'The Future of Universities: Past and Present', Rylands Lecture, Manchester, 1920.
7 DES, *Education: A Framework For Expansion*, HMSO, 1972, p. 30.
8 Charles Handy 'Missing Ingredient', *Times Higher Education Supplement*, 10 March 1989, p. 26.

9 For an excellent summary of competing definitions of transferable skills see, Alan Smithers and Dianne Parker, *What employers want of higher education: a review of the evidence*, MSC, 1988, pp. 45–55.

7

Industry and Higher Education: A Strategy for Partnership

Geoffrey Harding and Brian Kington

Twenty-five years ago, a review of partnership between industry and education would have begun by arguing the reasons for the sectors to work together. Later a number of independent observers[1] identified as a major cause of our industrial decline in the economic league table the lack of esteem for wealth-creation. This was fostered and given substance by an educational system which valued the intellectual at the expense of the practical, the thinker rather than the doer. Today the mutual dependence of industry and education is accepted, at least in principle, even if this is not always manifested in practice.

Industry and commerce need the help of education in providing qualified manpower and allowing research expertise to flourish; education requires a healthy economy to provide its resources. Opinion leaders from both sectors have responded in movements such as Education for Capability and the Council for Industry and Higher Education, and a major national campaign was launched in Industry Year in 1986 and developed further in 'Industry Matters' to focus attention on the issues and the need for action.

Industry's motivation for contributing to this growing partnership is varied: image in the marketplace, access to valuable research, combating skills shortages, fulfilling a responsibility to the community. This diversity often results in a variety of responses with, even in one organization, several players participating each with their own objectives.

In this paper, a case study is presented of how one high-technology company engages in partnership with higher education: the reasons for our participation, our objectives and, through examples of our programmes and activities, how we attempt to realize these objectives. More importantly, it explains how we have developed a management process to ensure a cohesion and synergy between the various interests in a large organization to make the best use of our resources and to present a clearer picture to our educational partners.

Building a framework

As a framework, we have focused on four areas of direct interest to IBM – recruitment and training, research relationships, market development and

Figure 7.1   Analysis of company interests by education sector

	Policy	Recruitment and training	Research links	Market development	Corporation social responsibility
Schools, 5–16	Yes	No	No	Yes	Yes
Education and training, 16–19	Yes	Yes	No	Yes	Yes
Higher education	Yes	Yes	Yes	Yes	Yes
Adult and continuing education	Yes	Yes	No	Yes	Yes

corporate social responsibility – each of which has its own specific educational needs and has over a period of many years developed its own relationships with the sector. In this, our interests are similar to those of many other organizations with well-established education programmes. Underpinning these individual needs is our contribution to the broader national policy decisions on, for example, the curriculum or research. In our overall planning, each area of interest is examined by educational sector: schools, 5–16; education and training, 16–19; higher education; adult and continuing education. The matrix shown in Figure 7.1 illustrates the coverage of these by the company as interests. In this example, we shall concentrate on the higher education sector.

Unfortunately, neither company nor educational organization is sufficiently delineated to allow this ideal, compartmentalized picture. In all our interests, for example, we are likely to have an influence on the curriculum, either directly or indirectly, while projection of the company image is achieved at all the intersections. Similarly, changes in the schools examination system, either at A level or at a younger age, will have an impact on teaching in higher education. Nevertheless, this simple model is a useful guide in analysing our activities and identifying areas of overlap.

Management of issues

As a next stage, national education and training issues are reviewed and, where possible, related to the matrix. From these we select those where we have a particular interest or concern and where we have the ability to contribute resources or influence decisions. Management ownership is then assigned and action plans drawn up. These will include objectives, company positions, development projects or sponsorship programmes and channels for delivering opinions. In order to ensure that the various players – personnel, marketing, research and development, public affairs – are complementing each other, action teams are set up to address educational sectors or specific issues. Finally, overall reviews are conducted periodically by executive management whose major role is to select priorities, approve resources and monitor performance.

Of the national issues, some may be specific to our own industry, for example the need to ensure that all graduates are competent to apply information technology or to contribute to the national debate on technical skills shortages. Such issues can in turn generate others. Related to skills shortages, we have an interest in encouraging wider access to higher education, in releasing the latent resources of groups with low participation (women, ethnic minorities and the disabled), and in emphasizing the need for continuing education and retraining to enable people to adapt to the rapid changes in technology.

More broadly, and often in concert with other companies, we will attempt to ensure that the curriculum in higher education addresses both the specific technical needs of industry and commerce and the general capabilities required: communication skills, the ability to work with others, leadership, personal enterprise, and above all, the fostering of a positive attitude towards wealth-creation. Industry is also expected increasingly to participate in the management and funding of higher education and research, to share its skills in personal and financial management with the education sector, to provide industrial governors for polytechnics and colleges, to engage in joint research or to assist with student maintenance.

These examples illustrate the breadth and diversity of the national policy issues on which a company may be required to take a position, representing itself, a sector of industry or even industry and commerce in general.

Interest areas

Turning to the individual areas of interest, the reasons for partnership are usually narrower, the company objectives more easily defined and measurement of achievement easier to identify and quantify. In *recruitment* of graduates, numbers required and the associated skills mix are defined for each year, and the objective is simply to achieve the quality and quantity of graduates for IBM's needs. A close relationship with and knowledge of individual departments, often supported by research links, can be a most effective vehicle for obtaining specialist skills, enabling a company to attract recruits through their direct knowledge of its technical interests and personnel policies. More generally, these contacts can be fostered by student programmes: pre-university and summer vacation studentships or employment during the sandwich period of a polytechnic course. As skills shortages become more serious, individual student sponsorship becomes more attractive. Equally importantly, those who are not recruited will hopefully carry a good impression of the organization in their professional careers which may bring them back into contact with it as customers or suppliers.

Higher education is also a valuable partner in helping a company in its internal technical *training*, not only in providing specialized knowledge and expertise but also, for example, in giving academic recognition and accreditation to in-company training. The benefits for this academic partner on gaining first-hand knowledge of the needs of the company and of the latest technical achievements have obvious benefits for teaching.

Research links are equally specific, enabling a company to enhance and complement its own in-house skills and, particularly in the case of high-technology industry, bringing the academic researcher up to date with advances in technology and the application of scientific research.

This two-way technology transfer is of particular value in interdisciplinary activities. For example, the application of computer technology, particularly graphics, to medicine at the IBM United Kingdom Scientific Centre, through joint projects between industry-based computer scientists and academic medical researchers, has yielded results well beyond the capability of either partner individually. Further opportunities are offered by joint supervision of research students and staff exchanges. In addition to the benefits of technology transfer and personal development, the company image is enhanced and clarified in a valuable audience of current and future decision-makers.

Research links are generally characterized by a strong degree of common interest between the partners and a concentration on pre-competitive activities. In the information technology (IT) industry, partnerships are an established method of *market development*. Here, the user and manufacturer work together to mutual benefit to provide IT solutions for the user's problems. One of the most familiar examples is given by the automation of banking, but IBM has also extended this to higher education, working through the medium of study contracts to explore the application of IT to teaching, research and administration in higher education.

The final area of interest covers *corporate social responsibility*; the concept that a company, like any other citizen, should play a role in the community beyond the mandatory payment of taxes. This can be realized in a variety of different ways, ranging from sponsorship of the arts to help for the disabled. Within IBM, support for education is one of the priorities in this area. In its application to higher education, the issue for focus is the relevance of education to the world of work – to encourage and support IT literacy among students by application across the curriculum, to develop the personal and social skills necessary for success in later life and to foster a positive attitude towards industry and wealth-creation. The resources which can be deployed are varied: money, equipment, secondments and, most importantly, the contributions of individual employees often acting in their own time.

In this section we have described the framework within which we develop our activities. We now go on to describe in detail examples of our activities to realize our objectives, in the various interest areas.

Partnership in practice: some examples

Policy

Industry and commerce are expected increasingly to participate generally in policy-making and management in higher education through, for example, membership of the Resources and Funding Councils, or more locally, as governors of polytechnics. Other channels allow us, in partnership with other industrialists, to make our views known on specific issues more closely related to our own interests, such as research or curriculum content. Organizations giving this more focused attention include the Council for Industry and Higher Education (CIHE); the Royal Society of Arts (RSA); and the Foundation for Science and Technology.

The CIHE, originally an industrial initiative, is composed both of leading industrialists and academics. Its aim is 'to encourage industry and higher education to work together and to represent their joint thinking to government'.[2] The CIHE presents a common voice to government and other institutions on such issues as student funding, widening access and research strategy. The aim of the RSA Education for Capability campaign is 'to prepare students to manage their own lives and make a positive contribution to the economic prosperity of the country'.[3] The emphasis is on application as well as acquisition of knowledge, the development of personal and social as well as intellectual skills. The Foundation for Science for Technology was formed to promote science and technology for the benefit of industry in the United Kingdom. It provides an influential forum for the exchange of views and ideas across sectors and between disciplines through a flourishing lecture programme, often sponsored by industry and held at the Royal Society. IBM has worked closely with the Foundation on such themes as broadening access to higher education and the exploitation of science and technology. Starting in 1989, we are sponsoring a series of annual lectures on key topics in education.

Recruitment and training

Industry needs more and better-qualified people who not only can adapt in a world of rapidly changing technology but also can lead and direct change. IBM in its recruitment and training programmes and in its external support is helping to ensure that today's students are equipped with the skills necessary for this task.

IBM has an extensive student training programme. During their period of employment students gain experience of the world of work, learn new skills and receive competitive salaries. We consider this not only an important social responsibility but also a key link in establishing a relationship with young people, many of whom will hopefully become future employees.

Students employed at IBM fall into three main categories: pre-university; industrial trainees; and vacation employees. Students work alongside permanent staff, and perform a wide variety of tasks in marketing, finance, information systems, personnel, manufacturing and other functions of the company. Assessments by recent students of their spell at IBM are the following:

My year at IBM has developed my technical and communications skills in ways that will be of great benefit to me in the future.

I have learnt how to work as part of a team, I have gained in self-confidence . . .

IBM puts much emphasis on this student training programme. Currently over 1000 students receive some industrial training each year.

A number of companies place great emphasis nowadays on the provision of bursaries and work experience for students still undergoing their full-time education. IBM also has such a programme, though it is limited primarily to engineering disciplines.

It is worth noting at this point two examples of validation of company training, which illustrate new dimensions of collaboration. IBM and Portsmouth Polytechnic have worked together on an honours degree course in Computer Science. Over 20 IBM-sponsored students receive half of their degree points through their IBM internal training. The polytechnic supplies the other half of the points required. This is the first instance of validation by the Council for National Academic Awards (CNAA) for in-company courses.

The other interesting 'study while you work' initiative brings together IBM's manufacturing plant at Greenock and the University of Strathclyde. About 60 IBM employees are currently studying for a Master of Science degree or postgraduate diploma in computer integrated manufacturing (CIM) at weekly one-day courses held at the plant and operated by the university. It is believed that this is the first time a university has offered to run a degree course, with open entry, at an industrial location.

An extensive, in-house technical professional development programme has been instituted to cope with our own upgrading needs. To implement this, we have called on assistance from our academic partners in specialized areas. But this is not a one-way process, since research and teaching in higher education gain first-hand experience of the latest technological advances and applications in industry.

Research links

IBM has many links with academia which seek solutions to problems of mutual interest and concern. Many of these projects are based at our UK Scientific Centre in Winchester, but several involve the IBM laboratory and manufacturing plants. For example, under the Government's Alvey programme, IBM and GEC worked together with the universities of Sheffield and Edinburgh on image recognition work. IBM and Cranfield Institute of Technology co-operated on a portable testing tool for robotic systems in manufacturing environments. A new edition of the *Oxford English Dictionary* was published in 1989 in conjunction with the Oxford University Press. Funds were provided for the European Academic Research Network (EARN). This enables UK academics to link up with their colleagues in Europe via the Science and Engineering Council Joint Academic

Network (JANET) network. EARN (European Academic Research Network) is also linked to BITNET, the US universities network.

The IBM UK Scientific Centre works primarily on how to improve human interaction with computer systems. This involves a considerable number of links with higher education, particularly in the areas of computer graphics, image processing and speech synthesis. Jointly sponsored research students and postdoctoral fellows work alongside IBM staff and representatives from other external organizations on projects of common interest. Through this work IBM not only contributes to the furtherance of scientific knowledge, but also ensures that its own technical staff are at the forefront of the understanding and application of IT.

A further joint programme is the Teaching Company Scheme, an initiative first developed by the Department of Trade and Industry and the Science and Engineering Research Council in the 1970s. This programme illustrates vividly the practical results which can be achieved in research and development through the active co-operation of higher education and industry. Graduates are seconded to a company for two years to work on a clearly defined project in association with the academic partners' staff as appropriate.

One such collaboration was between Brunel University and IBM Havant. This project commenced in 1985 and aimed to set up a highly sophisticated machining centre for machine castings used in the production of computer disk storage files. Both partners benefited enormously from this integration of skills to meet a common challenge. Further joint projects have begun between Brunel and IBM. Brunel has also several Teaching Company Schemes with other industrial partners. As the Prince of Wales said, in a speech to the Parliamentary and Scientific Committee in 1979, 'The Universities and Polytechnics contain much scientific and technological expertise which is useful to industry. The difficulty is to ensure that this flows to the right places in industry. The Teaching Company Scheme does just this.'[4] It is of interest to note also that all the graduates who participated in this joint venture are now working for IBM at its manufacturing plant at Havant.

Market development

As has already been stated, it is an established practice for manufacturers in the IT industry to join forces with users to solve common problems. The IBM Study Contract and IBM Institute programmes are examples of this type of collaboration, in this case with partners in higher education. Current study contracts can be found in such areas as: support for library systems; distance learning material for management education; software packages for engineering teaching; and production-control environment models. In all these joint activities a key objective is normally to develop some particular hardware or software which will be of benefit to both partners.

The IBM Institute sponsors teaching projects. These introduce students to new ways of using IT in the learning process. All projects attempt to break new ground through the development of applications and techniques in teaching. Major projects have taken place at the following universities in a spread of disciplines: Cambridge (engineering); Oxford (politics, philosophy and economics); Durham (geography); Southampton (history); Cranfield (computer integrated manufacturing); Imperial College (chemical engineering); and Manchester (management and business education). In all these cases equipment has been provided, often together with cash and people, to develop education software to enhance the teaching process and assist the teacher to add value to his or her role. The software is then made available to all other higher education institutions with similar departments.

Many other interesting joint projects are taking place in university and polytechnic departments under this programme. New education products have· been developed and thousands of students have been given the opportunity to become aware of the benefits of IT prior to entering their chosen professions.

Corporate social responsibility

We believe strongly that companies have a responsible role to play in the society in which they operate. There is a strong relationship between economic prosperity and successful business. We seek, therefore, to support those projects where we can make a meaningful contribution through the appropriate allocation of available resources – cash, equipment or personal involvement. We encourage our employees to participate in the activities and organization of their local education institutes. Some serve as governors, others as visiting lecturers or professors; others are involved in course design, case studies, and the provision of technical and managerial support.

Thus, when we plan our support programmes we look particularly for employee involvement, relevance to national issues and priorities and total commitment from our partners. Above all, we seek to make the most effective contribution possible based on all our available resources and skills.

Our extensive Lecture and Conference Sponsorship programme would come under this heading. These events allow academics and businessmen to come together in a less formal setting to discuss issues of common interest. One example is the IBM Annual Symposium. This takes place at a different institution of higher education each year and addresses the theme of how IT can improve the teaching process in a particular discipline or set of disciplines. Subjects covered so far include engineering (Cambridge, 1987), and management and business education (Manchester, 1988). In 1989 the Symposium will be held at Southampton University, the focus being on how best to exploit across the curriculum large volumes of information. Another example is the sponsorship in 1988 of the first national conference of the new movement, Women into Computing. Here we provided sponsorship in the form of cash and a female senior IBM manager as a keynote speaker. A further series of sponsored lectures is held each year in partnership with the Polytechnic of the South Bank. In 1989 the lecture will be given by Baroness Platt and address aspects of the engineering profession with particular reference to the opportunities which exist for women.

A note on secondments. A regular exchange of people between higher education and industry is most important in the forging of closer links. IBM seconds a number of its staff each year to work in academia, providing business and technical skills. One of the most notable examples was the secondment to Somerville College, Oxford, of one of our female professionals, Kittredge Cowlishaw during 1985–7 as a Fellow in Information Technology. Her role was to make the students more 'at ease' with IT and appreciate its benefits and applications before they pursued their chosen careers. Other current secondments in higher education are in research, administration, computer services, project management and curriculum development.

Finally, IBM has an extensive programme for the sponsorship of prizes and other awards at universities and polytechnics. For example, prizes are offered to top final-year students in computing and business studies at every UK polytechnic.

Contributions criteria

Even within the framework outlined, a company will receive many more requests then it can possibly meet. In selecting projects for support, the following approach has proved useful, based on a five-stage measurement process against pre-defined criteria. First, does the project address the broad issues mentioned earlier such as curriculum relevance, access, management education, IT literacy, the return of women to work, and so on? Second, can IBM contribute not just financially, but with materials, advice and particularly personal participation? The involvement of IBM staff in the organization, implementation or operation of the activity is considered important since it will help to cement even further a strong collaboration with our educational partners. Third, is the request under consideration in an area which we do not currently support? Fourth, how does it 'stack up' against a number of other selection criteria, such as national impact and priority, relevance to IBM's interests, dissemination potential, 'multiplier' effect (the extent to which a project's benefits could be replicated in similar institutions within academia), commitment of partners, quality of project and institution, and publicity value of contribution? Finally, a not unimportant factor, of course, is whether the contribution can be met out of the current planned budget?

Should the request for support prompt a favourable response to all these questions it often has to be finally allocated a priority rating against those other requests which also have reached this stage. Such a formal process is of considerable value when one considers the vast number of calls which are made on our not unlimited resources each day. This method of responding to support requests or proactivating the particular projects we may wish to become involved in is reviewed regularly. The criteria may be adjusted slightly to meet the changing education issues which are of interest nationally and to IBM at the time.

Conclusions and concerns

In this case study, we have described how one company is engaging in partnership with higher education. The strategies, policies and programmes reflect many features of the IBM environment: a relatively large organization with established management style and practices, a company both leading and experiencing technological change, an ethos which recognizes the company's and the individual employee's responsibility to the community, products which pervade all sectors of industry, commerce and domestic life.

A great many companies, in all sectors of industry, of all sizes, are making significant contributions to higher education in their own individual ways. Nevertheless, we hope our experience gained over many years is illuminating and of help to other partnerships. Our own relationship with higher education is still developing, particularly in response to changes in the external environment, but we believe there are certain key features which are essential to our strategy: the commitment and involvement of senior management; concentration on relevant issues; the application of a portfolio of resources (money, equipment, and, most importantly, the skills and experience of employees); a businesslike approach (setting objectives, allocation of resources, measurement of achievement, management review); and the involvement of all interested parties.

Looking to the future, some current issues are assuming greater importance and new issues are emerging. Access to higher education, stimulated both by industry's needs for more and better-qualified manpower coinciding with a demographic downturn, is coming to the top of the agenda, raising questions about the resources needed for an increased student population and the private sector's contribution. Expectations of industry, in general, are growing, not only in support of students, but also in research collaboration and involvement in teaching. This is not confined to higher education. Indeed, the calls for industry to contribute to school education are, if anything, even more strident. What is it realistic to expect industry or individual companies to contribute? As this contribution becomes a more significant part of educational funding, how can it be assured on a continuing basis? In times of rapid educational change, and since it is unlikely that all calls on our resources can be answered, what are the priorities for industrial support? How can industry's input and influence on the curriculum be more effective? There is no national curriculum for higher education and hence no obvious central mechanism. In our own IBM Institute projects, we have linked several institutions together. Perhaps the networking approach is an answer. Is it feasible to have agreed national aims and strategies, at least in outline, so that industry can be better guided? How can we achieve this and still retain individual enterprise and innovation?

It is obvious that any review can only be a snapshot of a rapidly changing scene. The encouraging feature of the present picture is that partnership between industry and education is now accepted as a mainstream activity, calling for discipline in planning and execution, and is not seen just as an optional extra.

Notes

1 M. J. Wiener, *The English Culture and the Decline of the Industrial Spirit, 1850–1980*, Cambridge University Press, 1981.
2 Preface, *Towards a Partnership: Higher Education – Government – Industry*, Council for Industry and Higher Education, Spring 1987.
3 Manifesto, *Education for Capability*, Royal Society of Arts, November 1988.
4 HRH The Prince of Wales to the Parliamentary and Scientific Committee, 21 February 1979.

8

Students: Partners, Clients or Consumers?

Victoria Phillips

The Secretary of State for Education and Science confidently predicts that by the year 2000 there will be 2 million students.[1] What kind of students will they be and what will be their impact on higher education in the United Kingdom? This chapter looks at the student dimension of higher education in the 1990s, and the challenges and opportunities these new students offer further and higher education.

Two million students

In proposing an expansion of further and higher education, the government is not only issuing a challenge to the education system to deliver the increased numbers, it is also forcing a re-evaluation of the nature of a 'student'. If a 'student' is to be defined as someone who studies full-time for an undergraduate or postgraduate qualification, then expanding numbers to 2 million would have such a catastrophic effect on the public sector borrowing requirement that the future career of the ambitious Secretary of State would be short-lived. If a 'student' is to be defined in a literal sense as a person who studies then the target of 2 million is realizable and not an economic liability. Include nursing education, professional skills, updating and companies' in-house training programmes and at a stroke student numbers are increased by hundreds of thousands. Of course, the easy way for the government to meet its declared target would be to include all post-GCSE qualifications in further and higher education statistics. After all, in the United States similar statistics are presented for participation rates, making it currently impossible for the United Kingdom to compare its participation rates with those of the United States. A simple sleight of the statistician's hand and all this could change.

Cynicism aside, if the target of 2 million students is to be met, what can also be predicted is that these students will not be 18 years old, with three A levels and predominantly male. The demographic time-bomb which is ticking away for employers will also affect the providers of education. For education to be a valued experience it will have to respond to the needs of older, more assertive students, people from a non-white ethnic background, people with family and work commitments and increasing numbers of women. For education to be valued by these groups it will also have to allow them not only into colleges but into decision-making structures and teaching posts. The challenge of 2 million students to the current rather smug higher education system, will be to see what, if anything, remains of the current system.

Students as consumers

Traditionally, higher education has been reluctant to see students as consumers of education. The 1987 White Paper[2] identified industry, commerce and the economy as the groups higher education had to serve. It failed to identify students and future generations as consumers of education whose needs had to be represented and responded to. The composition of polytechnic and college governing bodies specified in the Education Act 1988 shows all too clearly which groups education has now to serve, with industry and business having a decisive say. Industry and commerce themselves do not have a good track record on predicting the supply of employees nor their requirements from employers, hence the current somewhat undignified race to get former female employees back to the workplace! While students have never been positively encouraged to shape their courses (except in the most cosmetic fashion) the opportunities they now have even to have their views represented are almost non-existent. With one student representative on governing bodies and no representation on key decision-making committees, the poor consumer is merely expected to receive what is good for him or her.

What commerce and industry should know is that limitless amounts of persuasive advertising and cut-price bargains will not persuade consumers to buy something they do not want. The way commercial products are sold to a waiting public is by careful research of their needs and lifestyles. Universities, polytechnics, colleges and the government have all failed to research the future needs of students, and even when the implications of changed lifestyles (whether it be students with children, or students who have to work part-time to make ends meet) have stared them in the face, the methods of teaching handed down from the fourteenth and fifteenth centuries and Oxbridge colleges have been rigidly adhered to.

In recent months the Department of Education and Science has surreptitiously begun to refer to students as 'consumers'. There is a hidden implication in such terminology that those involved will have to pay directly for what they are consuming. The plans for student loans and fees are a clear manifestation of this; the associated idea is that their employer will have to pay for them. The consumer wants neither shoddy goods nor high-quality, but inaccessible, goods. For the target of 2 million students to be reached, higher education will have to shake off its elitism and become popular.

To become popular further and higher education will first have to define its new audience. Women, black and ethnic minorities and working-class people who are not represented in further and higher education in the numbers they are found in society are part of this new audience. They will not be persuaded to 'value' an education that does not respond to their needs either in the place or time where education is delivered, or in the curriculum or content of courses. How relevant do women feel is history which recounts the progress of men and ignores the essential contribution of women? How appropriate is the teaching of politics from a Westminster dimension which ignores the detrimental impact of racism and imperialism? How can engineering be taught without considering the influence of change on the lives of the workforce? Naturally, many courses already consider these diverse aspects, but do they say they do? Do course leaders and prospectuses present the contribution of women and ethnic minorities as an 'extra' or as central to the curriculum and content of the courses? Consumers will want to know. Unless they do, and unless they see the educational experience as relevant, it will never be popular.

As much a shock for the current planning mechanisms utilized by the University Funding Council (UFC) and the Polytechnics and Colleges Funding Council (PCFC) is the fact that consumers do not always want something because they are told it is good for them. Despite the most persistent exhortations from on high, there are still vacancies on engineering courses. Vicious attacks on 'Marxist' sociology degrees from media and Parliament alike have not reduced the enthusiasm of students registering for such courses, and general arts degrees still flourish. Voucher systems advocated by some vice chancellors would not help colleges plan their future student numbers, nor keep open unpopular courses, no matter what their importance to the nation's economy.

Treating students as consumers has other far-reaching consequences. Consumers who can withdraw their goodwill or fees at any point or exercise a consumer boycott, cannot be taken for granted. They will not put up with inadequate library facilities, or lack of tutor contact. They will take their custom elsewhere. Students could no longer be treated as a minor irritation in the 'serious business' of research and running an institution. Calling students 'consumers' is much more than just an adjustment of official language, it is a complete change in the institutional/governmental relationship with students.

Students as clients

Treating students as clients is something educational institutions are much more used to doing. Students as 'clients' are dependent on the professional expertise of the educators. That very dependence makes them less able to judge the expertise they are receiving and makes it impossible to compare one course or college with another, because one cannot place a monetary value on professional services. In a 'client' relationship much is made of the professional's relationship with his or her client, but the reality is that the relationship matters little as long as the professionals stick together. Doctors, solicitors and dentists consider it unprofessional to advertise their services or overtly to run down their competitors. The power remains fixed in the professionals' hands.

The education system will be at ease if in the future it has to treat students as clients. There will be no fundamental shift in the institution–student relationship. The student will continue to receive the 'best' professional advice, and if that advice is rejected then the student will bear the consequences. Of course, there are always other richer clients to pander to; research departments of major companies, the UFC and PCFC and the paymaster general, the government.

How will the new-style 1990s students respond to such a cosy 'client' relationship? Predictably, they will vote with their feet. As now, mature students will attend the colleges which not only actively recruit them but also are prepared to make a few allowances for them in the timing of their courses and in providing child-care facilities. The perpetuation of this 'client' relationship will not, however, mean that institutions which do not respond to new student demand will necessarily suffer. The institutions with the long honourable traditions and family links will continue to recruit via the old school tie, but they may get left behind, without the injection of new ideas and intellectual enthusiasm.

Students as partners

Government plans for increased fees and top-up loans will potentially mean that the student herself has a far larger personal investment in her education. The belief is that this will teach self-reliance and 'standing on your own two feet' values to the carefully cushioned children of the 1960s and 1970s.

There are many inconsistencies in the Department of Education and Science's (DES) approach. One is that the government's published figures[3] do not make enough money available for the predicted numbers of students in the year 2000. The panacea of the three access funds, with their proportionally tiny budgets of £5 million each per year, will not meet the needs of poor or otherwise disadvantaged students. Another inconsistency is that there is no evidence that people who are currently not continuing with education (either because the school system has turned them off, or because they cannot jump through the required hoops before being accepted on a course), are anxious to buy these opportunities. Government ministers claim that because we live in a credit-dominated society people are used to borrowing for future rewards. However, qualifications and long periods of study are not necessarily perceived to deliver rewards on a large scale. Furthermore, the clamour of opposition now coming from the banking community which is being expected to run the scheme (and, it suspects, subsidize it), may yet force a major government re-evaluation of its top-up loans scheme.

Notwithstanding these major inconsistencies in government argument, it may be assumed that in the future students may have a larger personal investment in their own future. Financial investment should give them a larger say in the quality and style of the education they receive.

Even without financial investment there are many advantages to institutions in treating students more as partners than as passive clients. In an era of educational expansion, student retention will become as important as student recruitment. Indeed, this is the experience of colleges and universities in the United States, where much energy and money is spent on making a college education an all-encompassing experience in order to guarantee student retention. Student facilities, sporting events and social activities are believed by the colleges to count as much towards student retention as the content of teaching. Treating students as mature people with a role in the whole educational experience both in the curriculum and outside will reap rewards for student retention and the future funding of institutions.

The treatment of students as partners in the education process should have started long ago. The higher education community would not now be in the position to complain that 'no one is prepared to defend us', if all the hundreds of thousands of graduates and ex-students in the community felt they 'belonged' to an experience they had gone through. Students do not feel much affinity to educational institutions once they have left. They have been treated like bystanders; no wonder there is no chorus of dissent when a system which has treated them shoddily is under attack.

Funding students

Whatever the nature of the student–institution relationship which is to develop in the 1990s, the funding both of structures and colleges has yet to be resolved. None of the funding models currently being floated meets the contradictory government intentions of vastly increasing student numbers and controlling public spending. None of the models allows planning of student numbers or courses. The hand-to-mouth planning and funding of further and higher education seem set to persist for the next decade with the consequent demoralization of staff, students and employers. The government has looked to examples in the United States to inspire the future funding of higher education. Allowing colleges to set their own tuition fees and encouraging them to raise funds from private industry and alumni are just the start of the process. What the government does not seem to have learned from the United States' experience is, first, the flexibility of their system, with course credits and time out built into the system; and second, their high drop-out rate. UK higher education may be expensive, but it is efficient. The US system is equally expensive (although the burden does not necessarily fall on the state) but it is also highly inefficient. From my own personal experience, I can testify that there are also other unattractive features of the US system, like the institutional poaching which goes on, with Ivy League universities talent-scouting high-flying students and tempting them away from their colleges with offers of scholarships, leaving smaller colleges with a constantly unpredictable intake.

Likewise, the favoured system of financing students through top-up loans with additional access funds has all the appearance of the muddled US system of financing students without learning the lessons of that system, with its inefficient delivery of funds to poorer students and the astronomical rate of default which has had significant implications for the US budget deficit.

The muddled thinking on funding, of both students and colleges, will continue throughout the 1990s. The students who need to be recruited to further and higher education to meet the ambitious 2 million target are not cheap. Some kind of incentive will be needed to persuade institutions to recruit such students. Equal opportunities schemes piloted in UK further education colleges and polytechnics have been shown to be effective but expensive. Unless these currently 'non-traditional' students carry some value-added bonus to institutions, sheer inertia will guarantee that they remain locked out of education and alienated from it.

Institutions which are geographically isolated and academically 'average' will be particularly vulnerable if they fail to recruit non-18-year-old students. The institutions who are inclined to rest on old laurels and traditions will not fare much better if they fail to respond to new demands from new generations.

Teaching students

Academic freedom is essential to the future of intellectually rigorous and attractive institutions. Decreasing reliance on government funds may mean less interference in teaching from clumsy legislation and planning measures designed to strengthen science and technology in preference to the humanities. However, new methods of funding may also bring their problems for academic freedom. Sponsorship from private industry may place conditions on teaching the values of social ownership. Money from transnational corporations may prevent teaching about the environmental implications of economic development. It is symptomatic that the National Consumer Council has recently been driven to produce guidelines on sponsorship in schools, to prevent large companies, particularly pharmaceutical and food companies, dictating the curriculum through the materials they provide for schools. How soon will such guidelines be required for further and higher education?

Other challenges of new students in education and a new relationship of the educational institution with them, will be concerned with the way in which teaching is currently undertaken. Part-time, block-release and evening students will not be bound by a rigid lecture timetable and irregular tutorials. Institutions may be forced to become open around the clock and around the year. Cuts in library spending and opening hours imposed from the early 1980s onwards will have to be reversed if libraries are to remain the laboratory of non-science students. Laboratories and computing centres will similarly have to extend their hours to respond to need. The venues of teaching will have to be considered, with peripatetic lecturers perhaps travelling between different workplaces and community centres rather than staying within the cloistered confines of institutions. Modular courses and credit transfer will have to be taken more seriously by all institutions if education is going to be delivered to new students with new experiences. Distance learning, using television, radio and correspondence will have to be built into courses, not considered as a sideline just relevant to the needs of Open University students. The keynote of these new methods of teaching will be flexibility. There will have to be flexibility in choice of mode of study – for example, to allow a student to start on full-time study then to transfer to part-time study, to allow her to take up some employment opportunity, and then to switch to distance learning when work takes her away from the college locality, and maybe even to switch back to full-time study. Flexibility also implies allowing students to take whatever time they need to complete the course. Just because our competitive education system now places a value on completing a course in three years precisely, this does not imply that a degree which a student has spent nine years attaining has less value. The intellectual snobbery which values high-pressured cramming will have to be replaced by a flexibility which enables students to go at their own pace and allow for changes in their circumstances.

Obviously there are some pioneering departments who already practice new teaching methods. The rest of the system will have to wake up to the needs of students rather than what the establishment says is best for them. Essentially the teachers will have to be wholly involved, with their experience given proper weight, training offered, conditions of service improved and morale restored. There will be 'new blood' among students and there will also have to be 'new blood' among academic and associated staff. People who over the last ten years have been deterred from academic careers will have to be attracted back and their non-academic experience drawn on for new flexible methods of delivering education to students.

In implementing new methods of teaching the needs of students must be responded to. Students whose views on teaching are rarely sought and even more rarely welcomed will have to be fully involved in planning satisfactory venues for teaching, acceptable systems of credit transfer and adequate child-care provision. The students should become the 'experts' and fully involved in the academic planning they have been excluded from. The 'centres of excellence' will become those places which allow the serious participation of students and do not seek to impose outdated and outmoded methods of teaching on reluctant, disinterested students.

Student participation and protest

Many of the challenges and opportunities offered by increased student numbers and new funding mechanisms will also have implications for traditional means of student involvement in education. Since the 1950s students as an organized group have been based in their communities – colleges, halls, or sites. Representation has been based in students' unions on one vote per student, and services have been provided for students by students on the basis of need, mainly for social and community activities. Amalgamations of colleges and multi-sited institutions have over the last 15 years provided a challenge for students' unions, a challenge which has been met with imaginative methods of student participation, and a degree of flexibility not normally reflected in their parent institutions. Students' unions have retained their influence by concentrating on the issues that unite students, rather than those that divide them. Student poverty (both individually and collectively) together with inadequate student services, libraries, and welfare facilities and transport have been powerful means of uniting the student body in institutions. The new dimensions of the 1990s will inevitably lead to a new diversity of students, each with different requirements from their representative body. Students' unions have been progressive in their thinking on involving their women members and black and ethnic minority members. They have been imaginative in their thinking by endeavouring to involve part-time and mature students. They would also be the first to admit that they still have a long way to go. In policy and practice, however, they are already streets ahead of many institutions.

Students' unions have always been involved in academic affairs and representing student views at academic boards and senates. They have, to date, exercised extreme caution when representing student views, in not jeopardizing other students' courses. This has always been a difficult task and the new dimensions of the 1990s will make it more so. The dangers of fragmentation of students' views when many students will not study full-time at the parent institution are considerable. Students' unions whose current influence is based on a discrete community will themselves have to devolve their decision-making and participation to ensure they are continually kept acquainted with the various problems being encountered by students on their courses. This academic role may become much more important than any commercial or social enterprises which are based at the central institution.

For students' unions, as with institutions, their response to new diversity among their members will be essential. If, by the same token, institutions develop new attitudes to students by treating them as consumers or partners, then as long as students' unions are continuing to represent and respond to their student members they will increase their own influence and importance. Institutions ignore their consumers, organized as a lobby, at their own cost!

Without doubt all these changes will result in a fundamental change in the nature of student protest. As wider pressure-group politics have changed and become more sophisticated, so may student protest. The tactics and strategies employed by students in the future will continue to be based on those things they share as students rather than those things which divide them. If student loans are to be introduced the unifying factor for all students may be to get the best financial deal possible. If credit transfer is to become widespread, national recognition will be required to ensure a credit has a value to the student. In this climate, the quality of the education received by students will be at a premium. It will be in students' interests to ensure that a rapid expansion in numbers does not mean a rapid decline in quality.

Students as consumers or partners in their education not only have more influence, they also have far more responsibility. Students and their representatives can be guaranteed to take that responsibility seriously.

New dimensions?

When gazing into a crystal ball in order to see the future of further and higher education it seems inappropriate to make any definite conclusions. The last 20 years of higher education have shown so many shifts and changes of attitude from both government and participants that the only safe prediction is that nothing can be safely predicted. If the prediction of 2 million students by the year 2000 is fulfilled, perhaps from the future this will be viewed as the culmination of the Robbins principle and era of expansion.

Many of the assumptions on which this paper has been based may not come to fruition. The approach of Kenneth Baker, as Secretary of State for Education and Science, of trying to force changes by exhortation may not succeed. Certainly his faith that young people will remain in further education until the age of 19 without any incentive, either in the form of an education allowance or grant or guaranteed job opportunities, may prove misplaced. The advocacy of student loans as a solution to the long-term problem of financing students may yet prove to be flawed when the banks and financial institutions join with those who rightly oppose loans on an ideological basis. Even if loans do not go ahead the problem of financial support for students will have to be tackled with more imagination than has been seen to date.

The new dimensions of the 1990s are not simply caused by the vagaries of a government's decision-making structure, but by demographic factors beyond any government's control, and by continual advances in technology and learning which will demand new skills for employees. The challenge for further and higher education is to remain relevant and attractive to students despite the speed of change.

Notes

1 'Baker's Vision for the Next 25 Years', *Times Higher Education Supplement*, 13 January 1989, p. 7.
2 Department of Education and Science, *Higher Education: Meeting the Challenge*, Cm 114 HMSO, 1987.
3 DES *et al.*, *Top-up Loans for Students*, Cm 520, HMSO, 1988.

9

Using the Media: Structures, Delivery and Control

Naomi E. Sargant*

It is increasingly difficult to be clear what constitutes 'higher education' and how and where it is provided or takes place and, therefore, to determine what will be distinctive about the changing role of the media in relation to it over the next decade or so.

It is interesting that the Education Reform Act 1988 defines higher education entirely in terms of descriptions of courses which are deemed to be above the level of courses normally taken at school or in further education. It is seen to be at a 'higher' academic or intellectual level than what precedes it. It is not necessarily structured in any particular pattern, over any particular number of years, nor does the content have to be studied in any particular way. However, the conventional expectation is still clear. Students are expected to go on from GCE Advanced level work or the BTEC National Certificate or Diploma to study for a first degree, normally in one go, normally in one place and normally in one subject or in an integrated group of subjects, and normally with substantial financial support from the community.

Under such circumstances, the media that academics and learners use to assist in the learning process are the conventional ones, print continuing to be the most significant. Most institutions of higher education can now add to this an array of new technological resources: audiotape, videotape, computers, video disc, and the like. Some will have access to closed-circuit television on campus, others may use microwave systems to take their own teaching to other sites. Learning systems beamed down by satellite now exist in a number of countries, some operating internationally.

The purpose of this chapter is not, however, to engage in an exhaustive description of the current state of the art and science of the media. It is rather to try to identify the changes which lie, some of them hidden, behind the structures of the media and which may help or hinder the pursuit of higher education over the next decade or so.

The media are, of course, in themselves value-free. They can be used to store

---

* Naomi E. Sargant has also published widely under the name Naomi Mackintosh.

Table 9.1   Matrix of diversification strategies in higher
education

Existing students Existing ways of teaching/learning	Existing students New ways of teaching/learning
New students Existing ways of teaching/learning	New students New ways of teaching/learning

or deliver or transfer knowledge of any kind. The 'medium' as far as education is concerned is certainly *not* the message.

The principles of diversification in business give the matrix of strategies in higher education shown in Table 9.1. By contrast with traditional face-to-face teaching, what the new techniques can do in particular is, first, reach *more* people than could be reached through conventional ways and, second, reach people who could not be reached through those conventional ways.

The Open University (OU), for example, tried to reach new students in new ways. It did not, 20 years ago, set out to rewrite the curriculum of higher education. As Birnbaum said: 'The Open University has begun with a fairly straightforward notion of subject matter which assumes that students have much to learn from an intact cultural tradition.'[1] It did, however, set out to demistify the content of higher education and make it open to everyone to see, removing it from its cloisters and placing it in the public domain of libraries, bookshops and the airwaves. The institution, as Harold Wilson saw it, was to be a rational reordering of the facilities of existing agencies of adult education combining with the technological capacity of the media. Obviously it would cost less than conventional institutions as it did not require vast capital sums to be spent on bricks and mortar. The key to the expansion of provision, as the 1966 White Paper made clear, was to be the active use of the full range of media for instruction: 'The presentation of courses will variously involve a combination of television, radio, correspondence courses and study and discussion and community viewing and study centres'.[2] All of these teaching media and others beside have since then been pressed into the service of the OU in the United Kingdom and of many other such systems in other countries. Most are also being used for similar systems such as the Open Tech, the Open College and perhaps the Open Polytechnic.

Access was not at that stage in the early 1970s a matter of much concern to conventional institutions of higher education. The task of reaching mature students in large numbers was left to the OU. Indeed, as late as 1978, the Department of Education and Science (DES), laconically recorded the fact that there was no evidence of any unsatisfied demand for part-time degrees![3] Indeed, the country chose *not* to expand its provision for the conventional age-group over the last decade and the bulge in the birth rate which had culminated in 1964 suffered 'a real diminution in opportunity'. Alan Thompson, then Deputy Secretary at the DES, who used this phrase, commented at the same time that he expected that this diminution in opportunity would go by largely unnoticed!

The point of this story is, of course, that we have now started to approach the forecast time when the decline in the birth rate is starting to be noticed by admissions tutors and by employers of potential graduates. The diseconomies of decline faced by the school system are now facing higher education, and the government, pressed on by employers' needs, is proving more liberal in keeping up student numbers than might have been expected. Filling available places, particularly in some subject areas, is likely to bring in more mature students as well as moving down qualification levels at entry and maybe even the social class origins of the younger age group.

There has, therefore, been no particular incentive in the United Kingdom to make more use of the media for conventional-age students for conventional degree-level work. Where the media have been of greater use has been in the area of distance and open learning and of adult training.

The OU did not, of course, merely adopt an open admission system, it also chose a modular credit structure allowing students to complete their degrees in a wide range of subjects. Not surprisingly, and with great benefit on both sides, many students found themselves wishing to use their OU credits either in lieu of entrance qualifications or to gain advanced standing for other degree courses elsewhere. The transferability of credit agreement between the Council for National Academic Awards (CNAA) and the OU in 1977 provided recognition of this increasingly valuable practice which was also being followed within a number of other universities. Increasingly the tidy vertically integrated degree structures of the past are changing into modular and more flexible patterns and movement is possible within and between systems.

At this stage, we start to see a bridge between higher education as it has been traditionally practised, the OU's provision of higher education for adults, and the development of continuing education. Whereas much traditional adult education has not been at any particular level, or tied to particular qualifications, many post-experience courses or continuing education courses are at levels which are indistinguishable from those of degree-level work. Distance and open learning techniques prove particularly suitable for busy mature and motivated adults. The Manpower Services Commission's (MSC) funding of Open Tech recognized this, though the programme eschewed the use of national broadcast media. Indeed, the MSC has made it a deliberate policy to promote open learning as a valuable and economic means of training adults. Though the Open Tech rejected the possibility of using national broadcasting, the Open College is currently using it and current proposals for an Open Polytechnic have raised the possibility of delivery of programmes by satellite. At such a point, 'narrowcasting' would probably be a more appropriate term than broadcasting.

So the move away from tightly integrated degree structures made available face-to-face at individual institutions and dependent on the experience of local academics, opens up the possibility of an increased use of a wider variety of media. Dependent on the nature and size of the audience and the content to be studied, the media can be cheap or expensive. Print still remains an invaluable aid, as Peter Montagnon reminded us graphically at an international symposium on global learning:

> The book is still the most flexible, the most potentially innovative and useful medium available after the human voice; you can write comments in it, flip backwards and forwards through it, find your way by turning down the corner of pages, or underlining it, which is more than you can do with a video-disc. You do not have to plug books into an electric supply, just into your brain and your finger.[4]

What was unique about the OU was that it brought knowledge into the public domain and made it available, often freely, but always relatively cheaply. It was able to use another major public service free at the point of use, the BBC, to deliver its broadcast materials on TV and radio. The arrival of new technologies and, in particular, the arrival of direct-to-home satellites is soon to change this situation. The duopoly of broadcasting, provided to the whole community in the Reithian public service tradition, is entering its final years. While new technologies will bring more choice and, it is hoped, more variety to people, they will also have additional costs attached which will increasingly fall on individual users rather than on the community.

The question of who pays and at what point in the process is indeed the critical one, and I have discussed it at length elsewhere both in relation to education and training and to the future of television.[5] At an earlier stage in technological development, many services could only be provided by the community acting together to fund provision of communal services designed for individual benefit and use. This is still true for the provision of many services such as trains, electricity and water. They have developed into monopolies, or near-monopolies of supply more because of their scale and nature rather than for any philosophical reason. (Whether they are public or private monopolies is, of course, a different question.) Other services which used to be provided communally can now be provided for personally – watches, washing machines, refrigerators, for example. We do not need now to use the public clock, the municipal laundry, or even increasingly, public transport.

The same is also effectively true for the provision of education and particularly for higher education as far as most people are concerned. Just as the arrival of new technologies will inevitably break down the monopoly of public service broadcasting, so that same arrival, it can be argued, will break down the monopoly of institutions of higher education, and indeed of much of post-school education.

When people had no other choice they had to watch what the BBC chose to transmit – usually very good, of course, and selected within the best paternalistic tradition. Similarly, learners have until now had little choice about what they are offered to study and how. Professions and educators have laid down the curriculum in detail, sometimes even specifying procedures and requirements which have little to do with the communication of knowledge.

Adults, however, now no longer have to go and study in a particular location, over a particular time period and in a particular manner. They can use a variety of media in their own time and in their own place to continue their learning. The major barrier that has prevented this until now, that of accreditation, is being increasingly eroded. With transferability of credit, the addition of open and distance learning routes to many qualifications, the Open Polytechnic following on the heels of the OU together with such moves as the CNAA's credit accumulation and transfer scheme, the accreditation of experiential learning, competency-based assessment, and so on, there is every reason to suppose that many adults of all ages will prefer to study through such routes even if they have the choice. Many, of course, will not have the choice as the cost of full-time study will be beyond their means.

We come back to who pays and at what point in the process. Traditional face-to-face teaching is of course labour-intensive and its cost increases effectively in an arithmetic relationship to the number taught. Of course, some media are more expensive than others. The difference is that using the media is capital-intensive at the front end of the system. Once this investment has been made, the marginal cost of extra students is low in relation to the original capital expenditure. There is every incentive to expand the number of students so served both within the institution and in other institutions. And, of course, it is not necessary to stop inside national education systems. OU materials are widely used in other countries, even non-English-speaking ones, and the new Commonwealth of Learning initiative aims to capitalize on this same possibility.

As the communications village becomes smaller, satellite learning systems will make material available without respect to national barriers. The American National Technological University will, for example, beam courses to Americans in Europe.

There is, however, a down side to these developments. We have until now assumed that knowledge in all its forms is available and in the public domain for teaching and research. Indeed, it has been axiomatic that scholars will publish their new materials for colleagues and future generations. The most common form of publishing, apart from lectures, has been the written word, the most common repository being the public or academic library. These have been funded up front usually by the community and the user has not been asked to pay at the point of use. Of course, the question of copyright, of the ownership of intellectual property, has arisen, but not in a major way as the laws of copyright and conventions of royalty payments have been until recently adequate to deal with print publishing.

The media are used to store, transfer and deliver knowledge. When the medium is a book it is easy to store in an accessible place. Once published it has little continuing cost. Copies are distributable cheaply. New media which are increasingly being used to store knowledge instead of books, such as microfilm and data bases, are not as accessible, require expensive equipment to store and access and have a continuing cost attached to their use. It is ironic that just as librarians are endeavouring to open up more accessibly to a wider clientele, so the equipment of their trade has become more expensive, requires more guarding and is therefore likely to be less accessible. Some writers are taking an even more pessimistic view of the information revolution, the transition of information storage from the printed page to the electronic databank. It has been suggested that it poses the spectre of a new Dark Age: restriction of access to information by those who control the data banks.[6] An important reason for this is that it is the private sector that is building the most up-to-date data bases in such important and diverse fields as law, medicine and the natural sciences. While some can afford to access these data bases, and while the cost of packet-switching means that it does not matter whether they are in California or Switzerland, others cannot. Developing countries will be placed in an even worse position, with the gap between the information-rich and information-poor growing. Indeed, some information may be kept in private or governmental hands and not made available to scholars freely as in the past. In a related field, the pressing on the Third World by developed countries of, for example, the patenting of international life forms, and the private control of this intellectual property, constitutes a serious threat to international scientific research and is particularly damaging to Third World countries.[7] It is, of course, public libraries and academic libraries which have to bridge that gap; but increasingly they will not actually *hold* the information themselves. As commercial brokers of information do, they will move towards providing access to it rather than keeping it themselves: a scan of the keywords of specialist journals and copy of the chosen articles can be achieved very quickly, efficiently and relatively cheaply. However, it is the user who will be expected to pay. Ashton quotes Derek Law of Kings College, London, as endorsing the 'user-pays' principle: 'The issue is . . . whether universities and other public institutions should charge a commercial rate or cost price to its users.'[8] The catch here is that payment will need to be made for each use, and the same information may be charged for again and again. Information has become a commodity, and this moves its access further and further away from the assumptions on which the work of higher education is based.

It is not surprising that major print publishing companies such as the Maxwell Communication Corporation are extending their range of interests from textbooks and specialist journals to scientific and business software programmes and microfilm and online data bases – in fact, to any format for providing information which is effective and meets business needs. Whether in print or in newer technology, scientific and business information is now an international business.

Completing the circle of this argument returns us to the fact that much of the knowledge base of higher education is now being developed into individual learning packages for open and distance learning which are then available either for public distribution or commercial sale. The OU and the Open College both expect to market their courses. It is not surprising that a communications corporation such as Maxwell is interested in working with the UK polytechnic system to create an Open Polytechnic. Undoubtedly, this is an exciting project. The learning materials would be created by academic staff in individual polytechnics and, building on that base of knowledge and scholarship, would then be available for all the other polytechnics whose students may study or transfer as they wish across the array of expertise of all the institutions. At the same time, however, the implication is that these packages of knowledge will move from the public domain to the commercial domain, where they will be sold to private users and to overseas markets. The issue of the ownership and control of that knowledge and the copyright in it, given that the polytechnics are publicly funded institutions and are drawing on generations of public funded academic heritage, is a fascinating one.

Even if the knowledge remains in the public domain, there is, as noted earlier, an increased and recurrent cost attached to its continuing provision and use. An enquirer seeking information from the British Library online service (BLAISE) still needs to pay the cost of the telephone call, though he or she can economise by phoning in the evening!

Added to this trend caused by the move to new technology, is the general impact of the current philosophy of private ownership and the move towards privatization.

The dominant view at the moment, is that education and training are private goods to be privately paid for. The leaked Chevening papers make it clear that Robert Jackson wishes this principle of personal payment to have greater currency in the future.

> We have to make a basic conceptual shift from the idea of the government providing higher education through institutions . . . to an alternative paradigm of the government enabling individuals to purchase services from providers who are independent of government, but which are obliged to be more responsive to the customers thus enabled.[9]

At the same time, institutions of higher education are to be put under greater pressure to raise private funding.

Private funders not unreasonably have more interest in funding research relevant to themselves. This is certainly true of government departments, who usually expect to have the final say over the publication of 'their' research results. Will an increase in private funding therefore lead to a decrease in the quantity of knowledge reaching the public domain? Does the intellectual property rightly belong to the academic who prosecuted the work or to the funder who funded it or to the university or polytechnic where the work was carried out?

If whole sectors of education and training are to be removed from the public domain into private operation, how will intellectual interchanges and academic development take place? An immediate example of this is presented by the removal of much training from further and higher education to the new Employers Training and Enterprise Councils.

Not only are these local rather than national, but they are led by the short-term needs of current employers. Any improvements in the knowledge of the state of the art of training will now be in private hands, with materials being privately developed for particular purposes. Of course, employers may be philanthropic and share their best and most efficient training techniques with other employers. It is not, however, easy to see why the personnel department of Sainsbury's should aid Tesco personnel. Neither is it easy to see how the interchange of experience which would lead to improvement in theory and practice will take place in the future.

The increasing understanding of the value of intellectual property and its ownership is in tension in the field of higher education with the author's rights in his or her own work. The media increasingly have the power to make knowledge more accessible on a world-wide basis and the capacity to reach individual people breaking barriers of time and space, to the benefit of all in higher education. At the same time, the information revolution places the control of that knowledge and its availability within frameworks which will erect new barriers to its access and increasingly remove it from the public domain of scholarship and research. Higher education needs to ensure that governments nationally and internationally act to safeguard the freedom of access to information taken for granted in the past if it is not itself to become 'information-poor'.

Notes

1 N. Birnbaum, 'A View from New England' in J. Tunstall (ed.), *The Open University Opens*, Routledge and Kegan Paul, 1974.
2 Department of Education and Science, *A University of the Air*, HMSO, 1966, para. 8.7.
3 DES, *Higher Education into the 1990s*, HMSO, 1978.
4 P. Montagnon, 'Is There A Message in the Medium?' in Alan Thomas and Edward Ploman (eds), *Learning and Development*, Ontario Institute for Studies in Education, 1986.
5 N. Sargant, 'Learners and Television', *Journal of the Royal Society of Arts*, April 1987.
6 C. Ashton, 'The Growing Cost of Information', *Global Business*, Autumn 1988.
7 *Facts in Focus*, BBC Radio 4, 2 February 1989.
8 Ashton, 'Growing Cost'.
9 R. Jackson, 'Chevening Discussion Papers', *Education*, 4 November 1988.

10

1992: Higher Education and the Challenge of the Single European Market

Diana Green

The idea of creating a united Europe is not new. While its political origins are difficult to date precisely, the economic impetus can be traced to the immediate post-war years. This was initially translated into a number of treaties whereby heads of European states and governments undertook to rebuild the European economy by collaborating in the development of key basic industries such as coal, iron and steel, and nuclear power. A further step was taken in 1957 when six countries (Belgium, West Germany, France, Italy, Luxembourg and the Netherlands) signed the Treaty of Rome, committing themselves to the establishment of a single European economy based on a common market. The task of the Community was, 'to lay the foundations of an ever-closer union among the peoples of Europe' and 'to ensure the economic and social progress of their countries by common action to eliminate the barriers which divide Europe'.[1]

Attempts to dismantle these barriers have fallen foul of technical and political difficulties. Whether this is explained by a failure of policy instruments or is indicative of a more deep-seated failure to agree on a common approach to overcoming national differences is a moot point. Certainly, political will came increasingly under strain during the 1970s when the economic recession stimulated a resurgence of nationalism. Member states increasingly sought to protect their national markets not only from non-EC competitors but also against each other.

During the 1970s and 1980s, the EC has expanded and now comprises 12 member states ranging in size from Luxembourg, with a population of 367,000, to West Germany, with over 60 million. However, it remains a fragmented rather than a single market. Even the largest of these markets is less than half the size of that of Japan and a quarter that of the United States. It therefore became clear to member states that if the EC was to respond to the economic and industrial challenge posed by these world powers, a single European market was needed. In 1985, the European Commission produced a White Paper which set out proposals for achieving a more unified internal market and a clear timetable for action.[2] Eschewing a minimalist approach, it set out an agenda for comprehensive reform: identifying many of the physical, technical and fiscal barriers which prevented the free functioning of the market, it included more than 300 legislative proposals needed for their removal. The timetable for implementation of this radical strategy was tight: the reforms should be completed by the end of December 1992.

The Single European Act, which came into force in July 1987, provided the political impetus and the legal framework necessary for the achievement of a truly unified market. This wide-ranging Act amended the original treaties in specific areas such as economic and social cohesion and changed the voting procedure in order to speed up the policy-making process, providing for decisions by qualified majority rather than unanimity. Perhaps more importantly, member states recommitted themselves to working towards *political* union as well as economic union within Europe.

Much governmental and media attention has understandably focused on the challenge of 1992 for industry. Attempts by committed Europeanists such as the President of the Commission, Jacques Delors, to discuss the political and social implications have proved to be more contentious, as the UK Prime Minister's Bruges speech in September 1988 demonstrated.[3] This paper examines one policy area which is crucial to the successful establishment of 'a people's Europe', higher education. It discusses the structural, cultural and technical barriers to the internal market which currently exist, examines some of the measures designed to improve the mobility of staff and students within the European higher education market and indicates what further actions need to be taken.

Barriers in the higher education market

Higher education, defined here as advanced-level education for students of 18 and over, provides a useful case study of the problems facing the EC in achieving its aim of a unified market by the end of 1992. Diversity rather than unity is the hallmark of the current European system. Higher education structures, policies and provision vary, reflecting the historical, political and cultural traditions of the individual member states. While some sort of binary system is common, with universities providing more 'academic' courses and non-university institutions concentrating on more 'vocational' provision, there is considerable diversity even within this classification. In West Germany, technical and comprehensive universities coexist with the more traditional university institutions and alongside a number of non-university higher education institutions, including the Higher Technical Colleges (*Fachhochschulen*), providing shorter and more practically orientated courses especially in engineering and commerce.[4] In Italy, higher education is provided mainly in the universities or university institutes. The only separation of 'vocational' from academic provision is in specialized academies for fine art, the performing arts and physical education. A reform of the educational system of the Netherlands in 1986 has produced a system which superficially resembles the UK model. Alongside the universities, which account for about 42 per cent of provision, are 85 Higher Education Colleges (HBOs) providing vocational courses. The HBOs account for 50 per cent of higher education provision, have a higher proportion of part-time students and have begun to challenge the universities' monopoly of research, specializing in applied research.[5]

Other important national differences are found in ownership and funding. While in most member states the bulk of higher education is provided through state-maintained institutions, private sector institutions, including religious foundations, may also play an important role. In France, for example, higher education is provided by state-financed universities, Catholic universities, and a number of specialized institutions, some of which are privately owned and funded. France also proves the exception to the general rule which accords the academic universities in most European countries a higher status than the non-university institutions of higher education. The so-called *grandes écoles* train the intellectual (and social) elite for top jobs in business, politics and public service. Some, such as the prestigious Ecole Polytechnique, specializing in engineering, and the Ecole Nationale d'Administration, which trains for public service, are more highly esteemed than the universities. Many are financed and controlled by the central government. Entrance is highly competitive, normally involving a two- or three-year preparatory course following the school-leaving certificate (*baccalauréat*).

The diversity in national approaches can be illustrated by examining provision for teacher training. In Italy, those wishing to teach in secondary education must, in addition to a university degree, pass either a further examination and practical test or achieve a post based on a combination of academic and teaching qualifications. All candidates are required successfully to complete a year of teaching apprenticeship. In West Germany, teacher training is related to either the type of school or the stage of education. Courses last at least three years, are followed by 12–18 months' practical training, and an examination must be taken at the end of each phase. University teachers must be academically qualified but do not need a teaching qualification. In France, teachers are civil servants and are recruited at different levels by competitive examinations. Secondary teachers must hold a variety of qualifications, including a first degree (*licence*) in their chosen specialism and a further teaching qualification. One such qualification is the CAPES, obtained through a competitive examination in theory and practice taken after one year of professional training. Those wishing to teach in a *lycée* or university study for a higher qualification, the *aggrégation*. Entry to the competitive examination after a one-year course is limited to those with a Masters-level qualification (*maîtrise*).

Legal barriers

One aim of the unified market is the free circulation of workers. Theoretically, it should be as easy for a British academic to gain employment in an institution of higher education in another member state as in the United Kingdom. However, currently that freedom of movement is constrained by a legal barrier. Article 48(4) of the Treaty of Rome provides that the provisions of Article 48 on the free movement of workers 'shall not apply to employment in the public service'. The Single European Act did not amend this provision. Consequently, in those countries where teachers have the legal status of civil or public employees, their posts are theoretically covered by this exclusion clause. In practice, there are two key factors; first, how widely the 'public sector' is defined, and second, what restrictions are placed on the public service function. The most crucial of these is *nationality*. In most EC countries, non-nationals are excluded from most permanent public service posts, including teaching. Exceptions to this rule vary from country to country. In West Germany, universities can employ foreign academics, while in France, which has the widest definition of public service, the only exceptions to the nationality requirement in education are short-term contractual posts in some universities and research institutes. In Belgium, it is possible for a non-national to hold a teaching post at any level only by Royal Decree. In the United Kingdom, the nationality rule applies only to a small number of strictly defined civil service posts. Teachers are excluded. Indeed, the 1976 Race Relations Act makes it unlawful to discriminate on racial grounds, including nationality, in relation to access to jobs and to conditions of employment. The Act specifically prohibits discrimination against non-nationals by public sector employers, including the local authorities, the education authorities, the National Health Service and public corporations such as the BBC.[6] In the United Kingdom, then, jobs in the education sector, including higher education, are open to nationals of other member states on a par with British workers.

The UK approach is not typical, as can be seen from one case which was referred to the European Court.[7] This involved a UK national who was refused access to a teacher training course in West Germany which involved teaching practice in a state school. The case was referred to the Court to determine whether the trainee teacher could be a worker under Article 48 and thence have legal entitlement to the activity or be excluded on the grounds that the post was a civil service post (i.e. fell within Article 48(4)). The Court decided that teacher training activity was not covered by Article 48(4) and that the principle of free movement of workers applied.

In response to growing criticism of the piecemeal approach by the European Court and the ambiguity of its judgements on this crucial aspect of worker mobility, the European Commission issued a statement in March 1988.[8] This set out a strategy for eliminating restrictions on the grounds of nationality to access to a range of non-sensitive posts in the public sector, including teaching in state educational institutions and research for non-military purposes. This statement also recognized the link between this strategy and other Commission policies designed to promote academic, professional and occupational mobility, discussed below. Before leaving this point, it is important to underline that while action is being taken to remove the legal barriers to *access* to employment in these areas, it is recognized that inequalities of opportunity may persist for non-nationals in respect of career progression. Member states are free to insist on the possession of national occupational and professional qualifications for specific functions, especially at more senior levels. Similarly, linguistic qualifications could also be specified, provided it can be demonstrated that they are essential for the post and not imposed in such a way that non-nationals cannot satisfy them. However, as Handoll points out,[9] the extent to which these become real rather than theoretical barriers will be determined by the level of *communitaire* feeling, i.e. the extent to which nationals from other member states seriously attempt to integrate into the host society.

Student mobility

For most member states, entry into higher education is dependent on the holding of a secondary school leaving certificate or diploma. Few outside the United Kingdom operate any additional selection process at the stage of entry. The periods of study needed to secure specific qualifications differ. In the case of a first degree, for example, it takes three years in a French university for a *licence* and four for a *maîtrise*; four years in an Italian university; four to seven years in a West German university (although students present themselves for examination when they feel they are ready!) and three to four years in a Higher Technical College; while students take four years to obtain a degree in a Dutch university and the same time for a vocational qualification in an HBO. In England and Wales the norm is three years although some vocational courses, such as sandwich degrees, last for four years.

The cost of higher education to the student and the extent and nature of student support also vary from country to country. In France, tuition fees are nominal. Means-tested grants or scholarships are available but at a lower level than in the United Kingdom. Parental support is standard, particularly since French students tend to live at home and attend their 'local' university or college. By contrast, Dutch students receive a basic means-tested grant (which covers tuition fees) and can 'top this up' by a loan based on parental income. Interestingly, in Italy self-support seems quite important: while there are no formal arrangements for part-time study, only one-third of students attend university on a full-time basis, the rest combining work and study.[10]

The most significant potential barrier to student mobility is language. Within the EC there are currently nine languages which have the status of an official Community language, namely: Danish, Dutch, English, French, German, Greek, Italian, Portuguese and Spanish. In addition, there are more than 40 regional languages, while immigration has added the main languages of the Indian subcontinent and Turkish.[11]

Most foreign language teaching takes place in secondary schools, although some countries have experimented with foreign language teaching at the primary level; for example, since 1987–8, Italian primary schools have been able to offer English, French or German from the third or fourth year. In all member states, secondary school children have the opportunity of learning at least one foreign language from the first year onwards. In all countries except Ireland and the United Kingdom, this first foreign language is a compulsory part of the curriculum.[12] A second foreign language is offered in most countries as either an optional or a compulsory subject and, in some cases, a third and even a fourth language may be available.

A recent analysis of modern language provision in Europe[13] revealed a number of findings. First, the most widely taught language is English (outside Belgium and Spain). Second, in the United Kingdom and Ireland, French is the first foreign language. Third, France and the United Kingdom are the only member states where it is theoretically possible to learn all the official Community languages. Fourth, English and French are the only foreign languages taught to large numbers of children in the EC. And fifth, a majority of children end their compulsory secondary education with a practical knowledge of at least two foreign languages only in the smaller countries, such as the Netherlands and Denmark (English and German), and Luxembourg (German and French). It is therefore clear that language teaching at the secondary level is not providing an adequate foundation for the worker mobility which the unified market should provide. In the light of the potential structural, financial and linguistic barriers identified here, the Commission therefore launched a series of initiatives designed to remove these barriers to a genuine 'people's Europe'.

Removing the barriers

The first actions taken by the Commission to promote mobility in education and training were in 1976 when it launched study visit programmes for academic staff and a pilot project to facilitate the transition from school to work. Further steps were taken in the launching of two important initiatives, COMETT (Community in Education and Training for Technology) and ERASMUS (European Community Action Scheme for the Mobility of University Students), backed by the governments of the member states and funded through the European Parliament.

COMETT

The COMETT initiative, which was launched in July 1986, was designed to strengthen co-operation within the EC between higher education and industry. This was to be achieved in several ways, including:

1 The establishment of a European network of university – enterprise training partnerships (UETPs) with a remit to co-operate in the development and provision of training programmes.
2 Transnational exchanges of trainees, including new graduates, university staff and staff in industry.
3 Support for ongoing training programmes organized on a collaborative basis between higher education institutions and industry in fields relating to the new technologies.
4 Multi-lateral initiatives for developing multi-media training systems.

The programme was initially planned to last for four years, starting on 1 January 1986, with a budget of ECU 45 million. The bulk of this funding (80 per cent) was scheduled to support the second and third measures, with 50 per cent of the total budget being allocated to the transnational exchange programme.

In July 1988, the COMETT programme was extended. The aims of this second phase do not differ markedly from the first, although there is perhaps more emphasis on initial and continuing training relating to technological applications and technology transfer. This second phase is due to start in January 1990 and extends over five years with a budget of ECU 250 million.[14]

ERASMUS

Where COMETT was intended to promote industry higher education links in the field of training, ERASMUS was specifically designed to promote the mobility of academic staff and students. The first phase of ERASMUS was launched in July 1987 with an initial budget of ECU 85 million over three years. The ERASMUS initiative adopted a similar approach and drew on the experience gained from the Commission's pilot programme for inter-university co-operation, launched in 1976. During the ensuing decade, some 586 joint ventures for staff and student exchanges were supported under this pilot scheme.[15]

Under the ERASMUS programme, the two main actions are: an extension of the inter-university co-operation programme (ICP) providing support for joint educational developments, programmes of intensive seminars and exchanges of academic staff; and grants to help cover the 'mobility costs' of students spending a recognized period of study (normally three to twelve months) in another Community country. In addition, funding was made available to support the establishment of a pilot scheme for the academic recognition of degrees and course units in a European Community Credit Transfer System (ECTS), the development of common curricula in the higher education institutions in member states, the establishment of university associations and consortia operating on a European base, and ERASMUS prizes for staff and students in higher education who make outstanding contributions to inter-university co-operation in the EC.

Analysis of support for projects in the first two years of the Programme's operation suggest an increasing interest in mobility on the part of both academic staff and students.[16] Both the number of applications and the total amount of funding requested increased significantly. In all, applicants requested three times as much support in 1988–9 (ECU 103 million) as in 1987–8 (ECU 34 million). During 1988–9, the ERASMUS programme provided support for 1091 ICPs, of which 948 involved student mobility and 214 an exchange of academic staff; about 13,000 students spending a study period abroad; and 1267 visits enabling more than 2611 staff members in institutions of higher education to prepare co-operation programmes, study aspects of the higher education system or give guest lectures.

In 1988–9, the total number of applications for support for ICPs was 2041, compared with 898 in 1987–8, an increase of 127 per cent. The amount requested was almost six times the amount available (ECU 52 million, compared with ECU 9 million). Of the total number of applications received, 1579, (77 per cent) involved a student mobility programme, 745 (37 per cent) a teaching staff mobility programme and 575 (28 per cent) a programme for the joint development of curricula. An analysis of the involvement of each of the member states in all applications over the two years shows that whereas Spain and Italy increased their participation rates by 7.6 per cent and 4.7 per cent, respectively, the UK participation rate fell by 8.6 per cent. A breakdown of the applications by academic discipline shows a similar profile over the two years. The main difference is a substantial increase in applications in the fields of agriculture, engineering and languages, and, rather surprisingly, a substantial fall in applications in the field of business studies. It is also noteworthy that the number of applications in teacher education remained very low.

Demand for student grants grew substantially over the first two years of the scheme with requests in 1988–9 being three times the available budget.

An analysis of the flows between member states of students for whom grants have been requested within the framework of ICPs produces some interesting results.[17] In most cases, there is real balance to be observed in respect of the 'export' and 'import' of students for each member state (Table 10.1). Only the United Kingdom is a 'net importer' of foreign students. To what extent this feature is explained by the 'popularity' of English as a foreign language and/or the financial attractiveness of the United Kingdom for the countries (increased as a result of the European Court's decision that EC students are effectively 'home' students so that their tuition fees are paid for by the UK government) is a debatable point!

Table 10.1   Student mobility within the inter-university co-operation programmes

Member state	'Exports'	'Imports'
Belgium	320	330
Denmark	120	113
West Germany	2056	1830
Greece	164	97
Spain	1056	970
France	2543	2587
Ireland	266	357
Italy	700	592
Luxembourg	–*	–*
Netherlands	530	489
Portugal	136	128
United Kingdom	2348	2851

* Figures too small to be significant
Source: ERASMUS Newsletter, 1/1988.

Table 10.2   Study visit grants: applications by member states

Member state	1987–8	1988–9	Increase (%)
Belgium	151	240	+ 58.9
West Germany	235	294	+ 25.1
Denmark	81	87	+ 7.4
Spain	297	488	+ 64.3
France	350	546	+ 56.0
Greece	149	289	+ 93.9
Italy	246	454	+ 84.5
Ireland	94	112	+ 19.1
Luxembourg	1	3	–
Netherlands	139	173	+ 24.5
Portugal	108	275	+154.6
United Kingdom	526	549	+ 4.4
TOTAL	2377	3510	+ 47.7

Source: as Table 10.1.

For the academic year 1988–9, teachers and administrators submitted 3510 applications for grants to visit institutions of higher education in other member states, compared with 2377 in 1987–8. Table 10.2 shows the number of visit grants requested by country of request and the rate of growth of applications with respect to the previous year. About two out of every three applications relate to a visit designed to prepare new co-operation agreements, underlining the importance of the study visit scheme to the ICP.[18]

The analysis of visits by academic discipline is also interesting. It reveals that the visits relate to fields of study which are less well represented in ICPs, while the fields of study which are already involved in the ICPs are proportionately less well represented in the visits (Table 10.3).

Table 10.3   Study visits in 1988–9 by field of study

Field of study	Percentage of ICPs	Percentage of visits
Agriculture	3.6	5.3
Fine Arts	2.08	4.7
Teacher Education	2.1	6.1
Humanities	5.5	7.5
Mathematics	3.6	5.7
Medical Sciences	5.8	8.6
Languages	18.9	11.3
Engineering	14.5	9.9
Business	9.4	4.7

Source: as Table 10.1.

Academic recognition of diplomas

The academic recognition of diplomas, defined as the recognition of higher education entrance qualifications, study periods, and intermediate and final qualifications which takes place inside institutions of higher education, is a necessary condition of student mobility in the EC. Given the diversified nature of the European educational system, the procedures relating to academic recognition are inevitably long and complex. A number of bilateral, multilateral and unilateral agreements between the member states already exist. For example, multilateral agreements cover the equivalence of diplomas leading to admission to universities (11 December 1953), equivalence of periods of university study (15 December 1956) and the academic recognition of university qualifications (14 December 1959). However, the process of academic recognition has, like attempts at harmonization in other policy areas, tended to be slowed down by the weight of technical detail and political haggling.

Progress was made in 1983 when the Education ministers of the member states agreed to make existing procedures more flexible and to improve the dissemination of information on this topic. In 1984, a further step was taken when the Community established a Network of National Academic Recognition Centres (NARIC). Under the ERASMUS programme, NARIC has been extended and consolidated.

It should perhaps be pointed out that although academic recognition features in only one section of the ERASMUS programme, it is actually central to the success of the whole ERASMUS scheme. Academic recognition is, after all, the prerequisite of any student's successfully completing part of his or her programme of study abroad. It is also clearly a foundation stone of any European university/higher education network. Another important measure included in this section of the ERASMUS programme designed to achieve the same objective is the decision to establish a Europe-wide course credit transfer system (ECTS). A pilot scheme was announced by the Commission in 1988,[19] spanning a maximum of six academic years from 1989. The scheme allows students enrolled at some 80 universities and other higher education institutions to study in more than one country and still obtain their degrees within the stipulated time period by receiving academic credits for course units, intermediate and final qualifications at one institution and continuing their studies at another institution within the ECTS system. The pilot phase covers five subject areas: business administration, chemistry, history, mechanical engineering, and medicine. Students enrolled on the scheme earn 60 credits for a full academic year and will have to accumulate 240 credits to obtain a degree, thus requiring four years of study.[20]

Harmonization of vocational and occupational qualifications

One of the barriers to occupational mobility identified by the Commission is the specific nature of diplomas, training certificates and other professional or practical qualifications recognized within each member state as giving access to certain occupations or occupational categories. Like the educational systems, vocational training systems vary considerably from one country to another. The Commission has therefore sought ways of harmonizing vocational and professional qualifications, including the development of a system of establishing comparability between vocational qualifications recognized by different member states, and the issuing of Directives aimed at facilitating the pursuit of occupations which are subject to specific conditions as regards training such as the health-care professions, engineering, architects and lawyers. In July 1989, the Commission adopted a proposal for a Council Directive aimed at introducing 'a general system for the recognition of higher education diplomas'.[21] This system is based on the comparability of university-level training courses organized by the member states and co-operation between national administrations to facilitate the assessment and definition of professional qualifications on the basis of higher education diplomas. The aim of the Directive was to facilitate access to the professions rather than establish a system of equivalence between university degrees.

From *ERASMUS* to *LINGUA*

It is clear from the first two years of operation of the ERASMUS programme that, despite its undoubted success in increasing the mobility of staff and students and promoting inter-university co-operation, participants have failed to exploit the benefits of the scheme to its full advantage, largely because they lack the essential foundation in terms of foreign languages. The Commission has therefore decided to recommend a new action programme known as LINGUA. The draft proposals make it clear that the overriding aims of the LINGUA programme are to increase the capacity of citizens in the EC to communicate with each other by a quantitative and qualitative improvement in the teaching and learning of foreign languages within the EC; and to ensure effective measures towards the provision, for the benefit of enterprises in the EC, of the necessary levels of foreign language expertise in the present and future workforce in order to enable those enterprises to take full advantage of the internal market. The approach adopted hinges on a diversification of languages on offer in education and training programmes. Its main thrust is in the vocational training field although it is conceded that action is equally necessary at the school level.

The proposal reflects and attempts to respond to the concerns identified above, that one of the most intractable barriers to mobility in the planned internal market is language. The LINGUA programme clearly complements the ERASMUS programme; indeed, there is an overlap for example where students are on courses where a substantial proportion of time is given to the study of a Community language. At the time of writing it is not clear how the two programmes will coexist.

The task ahead

The approach adopted in this chapter in examining the challenge of 1992 for higher education is to see it as a case study of the problem of adaptation faced by the Community. Since the aim of the EC is to create a unified market, the language used has been the language of economics rather than politics. It would be wrong, however, to assume that the starting point for the analysis was the assumption that education was a simple private good, like cars or computers. Theoretical debates about the nature of education and its provision are clearly outside the scope of this chapter. Nevertheless, it is important to make explicit two assumptions of the analysis which, in turn, underlie the EC's policy approach to 1992. First, the harmonization of the various educational systems within the EC and the removal of internal barriers are clearly important aims *per se*, but, more importantly, they provide a means of realizing the mobility of workers which is the policy objective lying at the heart of the plan to create a unified economic market. Second, the educational policies (including policies relating to higher education) pursued by the member states, acting both individually and collectively through the EC, are motivated by instrumental considerations. Education and training are seen as the prerequisite of national and European economic success. Moreover, they are seen not simply or mainly as a form of investment for the individuals concerned but rather as an investment on behalf of the national economy and the wider European economy of which the national economy is a part. While this instrumental motive may not be new, it has become increasingly explicit since the late 1970s, partly as a result of pressures in international trade and partly because of changing demographic trends within the Community.

In 1985, the population of the European Community was 322 million, representing 6.7 per cent of the total world population. However, the rate of growth of the European population is weak. Projections in 1985 for the next 20 years suggested a growth rate in the EC of less than 2 per cent, compared with 17 per cent in the cases of the United States and the Soviet Union, 8 per cent in the case of Japan and a projected average world rate of 36 per cent. Within Europe a demographic decline has already been recorded in West Germany and Belgium.[22] Within the global total is a worrying decline in the number of young people in Europe, resulting from a decline in the European birth rate since the 1960s. A recent report to the President of the European Community by the Round Table of European Industrialists,[23] pointing to the twin problems posed by this decline and by the spiralling demand by companies for trained manpower, warns that Europe is in danger of losing its technological edge in the absence of sweeping educational reforms.

The study, which was carried out with the help of 24 large companies from 11 countries, reveals dissatisfaction with the education system throughout Europe, especially when compared to those of the United States and Japan. In addition to the criticism of standards in primary and secondary schools, the report draws attention to the inadequate number of students in higher education taking technical subjects and, in some countries, to poor vocational training systems.

The dissatisfaction of the European industrialists finds an echo in the policies of some of the national governments, too. Thus, in Britain the 1987 White Paper identified the need for a more instrumental approach to higher education and set a target of increasing the number of students in higher education by 50,000 a year.[24] This was, in part, a response to concern that participation rates in the United Kingdom were considerably lower than European and international levels and thus likely to constrain future national economic performance. Similarly, at the beginning of 1989, the French government announced a five-year education plan designed to make the French the most highly trained nation in Europe by the year 2000.[25] The Jospin Plan is designed to reduce the number of pupils leaving school without any qualifications and double the number of pupils taking the *baccalauréat* (from 40 per cent to 80 per cent of school children) by the year 2000. The scale of the French government's plan becomes evident when these targets are compared with current UK performance: less than 20 per cent of UK pupils pass two or more A levels.

The Jospin Plan covers both secondary and higher education. The latter will clearly be affected by an increase in the number passing the *baccalauréat* (assuming the pass rate remains stable) since those who pass it are automatically eligible for entry to higher education. There are already 1.3 million French students at this level. Although the drop-out rate is higher and, as was indicated earlier, the duration of study is longer, this is more than double the number in the United Kingdom. The French government plans to increase this number to around 2 million by the end of the century. It is also worth noting that while both the UK and French plans for educational reform emphasize national economic needs, one explicit aim of the French education plan is to make the French educational system 'more open, in method and content, to international co-operation and the building of Europe'.[26]

The French are notorious for setting themselves unrealistic planning targets. And in achieving their national educational aims the French, like the British, face a number of constraints. In order to implement its planned educational reforms, for example, the French government estimates that it needs an additional 290,000 primary and secondary teachers and 70,000 university teachers by the end of the century. However, as in the United Kingdom, there has been a progressive decline in the pay of French teachers and a deterioration in their conditions of service and professional standing relative to other occupational groups. This has led to demoralization within the profession which has, in turn, made recruitment difficult. In secondary education in both the United Kingdom and France shortages in key subjects such as maths, science and languages are becoming critical. In both countries, the government's plans for reforming and expanding educational provision are being undermined by the inability to recruit and retain the professionals on which the service depends. In both the United Kingdom and France, demoralization has been underlined and exacerbated by worsening industrial relations and threats of industrial action. In the United Kingdom, a further indicator is the increase in the 'brain-drain' during the 1980s. While the net effect of the exchange of academics is, according to government statistics, small (being offset by inflows from abroad), the loss of some of the most distinguished British academics to countries such as the United States, Australia and New Zealand is clearly a loss to both the United Kingdom and the wider European Community.[27]

The responses of the UK and French governments to the challenge of 1992 are, by definition, national responses, motivated by concern about national economic performance within the European and wider international economy. What tasks still face the member states collectively, within the Community? The report of the Round Table of European Industrialists prepared for the Commission referred to above claims to be the most extensive investigation of education on a Europe-wide basis. Among its recommendations for reform are several which have already been discussed in this chapter such as the transferability of degrees and professional qualifications across boundaries and the recognition of professional competence in work by the award of credit towards university degrees. Significantly, the industrialists argue for closer links between education and industry and suggest that industry's influence on curricula and qualifications should be increased. The most radical proposal is for a Europe-wide educational system with common core curricula, covering subjects such as maths and sciences, to encourage the free movement of labour. This system should be underpinned by a European educational television network. The establishment of a European Open University should also be explored.

Clearly, the infrastructure and the technology needed to underpin some of these proposals already exists in the shape of some of the initiatives discussed above, such as the NARIC and the ECTS. The major obstacles to their achievement are financial and political. It is to be hoped that higher education does not fail to respond to the challenge of 1992 because of arguments about who should pay or because of the failure of national governments to agree on what kind of Europe they are attempting to construct. Perhaps the greatest challenge that higher education faces is the task of enabling students to take full advantage of citizenship of the wider European political community.

Notes

1 Treaty setting up the European Economic Community (Rome, 25 March 1957), HMSO, 1967.
2 European Commission, *Completing the Internal Market*, EC Commission, 1985.
3 *The Single European Act* (*Acte Unique Européen*) was signed by all twelve members of the European Community in February 1986.

4 Department of Education and Science, *Selected National Education Systems*, HMSO, 1985.
5 Olga Wojtas, 'The Centre's Final Curtain', *Times Higher Education Supplement*, 24 February 1989.
6 John Handoll, 'Article 48(4) EEC and Non-national Access to Public Employment', *European Law Review*, no. 4, 1988, pp. 223–41.
7 *Lawrie-Blum* v *Land Baden-Württenberg*, European Court case 66/85, 1987.
8 *Official Journal of the European Community*, 18 March 1988.
9 Handoll, 'Article 48(4)'.
10 DES, *Selected National Education Systems*.
11 'The Teaching of Modern Languages in the European Community', *Social Europe*, no. 2, 1988, pp. 34–8.
12 In the case of the United Kingdom, a change of policy, included in the Education Reform Act 1988, means that a compulsory foreign language will be included as a foundation subject in the new national curriculum.
13 'The Teaching of Modern languages'.
14 *Bulletin of the European Communities*, nos 7/8, 1988.
15 'ERASMUS – An Investment in the Future of the Community', *Social Europe*, no. 3, 1987, pp. 34–7.
16 'ERASMUS Grants for 1988/89 Announced', *ERASMUS Newsletter*, no. 1, 1988.
17 Ibid.
18 Ibid.
19 *Official Journal of the European Community*, 27 July 1988.
20 'Higher Education without Frontiers', *Target 92*, no. 8, 1988.
21 'Proposal for a Directive on a general system for the recognition of higher education diplomas awarded on completion of vocational courses of at least three years duration', COM (86) 257 final of 7 May 1986.
22 *L'Europe en chiffres*, Office des Publications Officielles des Communautés Européenes, Luxembourg 1988.
23 *Education for Life: A European Strategy*, Report prepared by a Round Table of European Industrialists for Jacques Delors, Butterworths 1989; see also David Thomas, 'European education said to need urgent reform', *Financial Times*, 2 February 1989.
24 DES, *Higher Education: Meeting the Challenge*, Cm 114, HMSO, 1987.
25 Diana Geddes, 'France's No. 1 Priority', *Education*, 9 December 1988; Diana Geddes, 'France's Day of Glory', *Education*, 3 February 1989; John Izbicki, 'Echoes from across the Channel, as France Forges New Reforms', *The Independent*, 19 January 1989; Patrick Marnham, 'French Planning to be the Brains of Europe', *The Independent*, 19 January 1989.
26 Adriana Adrey, 'Fair exchange or academic robbery?', *The Independent*, 2 March 1989.
27 'Fair Exchange or Academic Robbery', *The Independent*, 2 March 1989.

11

Prospects for Higher Education Finance

Gareth Williams

The Education Reform Act and its aftermath

There will be three main influences on the funding of UK higher education during the next decade. Two result from government policy, the Education Reform Act, that completed its passage through Parliament in the summer of 1988 and the White Paper on top-up loans for students[1] which was published in November of that year. However, more far-reaching than either of these will be the effect of demography.

The Education Reform Act has four provisions which directly affect the funding of higher education. They are, in order of the extent of their likely influence on the long-term development of British higher education: the removal of polytechnics and most colleges of higher education from local authority control; the replacement of the National Advisory Body (NAB) for Public Sector Higher Education by a Polytechnics and Colleges Funding Council (PCFC); the replacement of the University Grants Committee (UGC) by a Universities Funding Council (UFC); and the abolition of life-tenured appointments for all new academic appointments to universities. Interestingly, the amount of attention each received during the passage of the Bill through Parliament was exactly in the reverse order, which says something about the continuing domination by university interests of the public debate.

The life-tenure of academic staff raises more than financial issues. However, financial aspects were undoubtedly uppermost in the mind of the government which forced the measure through Parliament, and universities and their academic staffs have undoubtedly used and abused tenure to their financial advantage in the past. Much misleading rhetoric was employed on both sides. During the period of rapid expansion tenured appointments came to be used in many universities as the dominant form of employment contract for academic staff. Young lecturers in their mid-twenties were given contracts for life, often after single interviews and only loosely supervised probationary arrangements. When financial stringency began to affect universities from the late 1970s onwards many of them almost ceased to make tenured appointments. Instead new staff were offered a series of fixed-term appointments and in many cases were required to sign away their statutory rights to redundancy pay when their contracts came to an end. Tenure was used by universities as an excuse for dragging their feet over restructuring in the mid-1980s, yet a very considerable amount of restructuring did take place and for the most part the cost of compensating tenured staff for early retirements was no greater than that paid to those forced out of colleges of education during the reorganization of teacher training a decade earlier.

The right of university teachers to a contract for life has now been abolished by the government for all new appointments. It is not clear, however, that the legislation prevents a university from offering a specific contract for a period corresponding to the working life of a particular individual and it is to be hoped that when the present period of severe financial stringency comes to an end universities will again be willing to offer what will be in effect tenured contracts to their outstanding scholars as is done in many US universities. Whether the abolition of tenure based on university charters and statutes will make any real difference to university employment will not be known for several years as it is unlikely that an individual recently appointed will be on any list of potentially redundant staff. By the time the new legislation does begin to have some effect, and university charters are revised to make redundancy of existing staff possible, higher education will have entered a new period of staff shortages and redundancy will once more become an academic issue.

The substitution of the UFC for the UGC is likely to prove to be a matter more of form than of substance. The main features of the UGC were that it was dominated by academics and its chairman was a distinguished university academic, that its grants to universities were mainly general rather than earmarked for specific purposes (though this principle has often been breached in recent years), and that it has been the principal source of advice to government on the financial needs of universities. There are to be some changes in all of these under the new arrangements.

The UFC has a larger proportion of its members from outside the universities. Its first chairman is the head of a college from outside the traditional university system. It is expected to have a less prominent role than the UGC in advising the government on universities' financial needs.

The principal constitutional changes are that, unlike the UGC, the UFC is a statutory body; the Council itself, not the Secretary of State, will be formally responsible for the allocation of funds to individual universities; and at least six of the Council's 15 members must come from outside higher education, a larger proportion than has been the case with UGC membership.

Under the new arrangements the Secretary of State will provide funds to the UFC for distribution to the universities. He may attach conditions to the money, but these may not relate to the funding of a named university. Decisions on how much to allocate to each university will be entirely for the UFC, which will be allowed to attach conditions to its funding of individual universities. However, these may not relate to funds from other sources. Where conditions are imposed by the UFC they ought to be subject to consultation either with individual universities or a representative body.

The PCFC has a structure, membership and mode of operation similar to that of the UFC. It will have responsibility for the 29 polytechnics in England together with 50 or so other major colleges of higher education. The similarity between the PCFC and the UFC will be considerably increased by the fact that all of these institutions under PCFC control are to be taken out of local authority control and transformed into independent organizations with a corporate status similar to that of universities.[2]

It is not, however, the establishment of new funding councils, nor their membership and constitution, which are likely to have the biggest effect on the funding of higher education institutions. The important question is how they will function when they come into operation and this is unlikely to be apparent for at least a year or two. During its first year of operation the PCFC will be dominated by the need to ensure that the transition of polytechnics and colleges from local authority control to corporate status proceeds as smoothly as possible. Their controversial decision to rescind the third round of NAB initiative grants can be seen in this light. The UFC shows every sign, for at least the first year, of maintaining continuity with the increasingly selective and interventionist policies of the UGC in recent years.

However, as the decade of the 1990s proceeds there certainly will be changes. One matter which has excited a certain amount of comment is how long the two separate funding councils will last. Many observers expect convergence and, well before the end of the decade, a merging of the two bodies into a single higher education funding council. Certainly this is a possibility and it is clearly going to be necessary for them to co-ordinate their policies on several issues. However, it is equally possible to foresee the two councils having very different preoccupations. The universities as a whole could well move up-market into activities related to research and research training while retaining their position as relatively exclusive suppliers of undergraduate courses to the better-qualified school leavers. At the same time, the polytechnics and colleges could become much more active in all aspects of continuing education, including access courses and a wide variety of training and retraining activities for employers. For a middle band of school leavers they might aim to offer good-quality professional and paraprofessional courses, of which teaching and nursing are two examples that are likely to have very rapidly growing needs for several years.

The second area of speculation is the criteria the funding councils will use in their allocations to the universities, polytechnics and colleges. In the White Paper which preceded the Education Act the government made it clear that it was expecting some form of contracting between the funding bodies and their client institutions.[3] Political discussion of funding through fees and vouchers led some commentators to claim that the idea of contracts is dead. However, in a letter to the Chairman of the PCFC on its incorporation in October 1988 the Secretary of State wrote:

I shall look to the Council to develop funding arrangements which recognise the general principle that the public funds allocated to polytechnics and colleges are in exchange for the provision of teaching and research and are conditional on their delivery . . . it will be for the Council itself to devise appropriate means of allocating funds between institutions. I shall, however, expect to see two key features. The first is a means of specifying clearly what polytechnics and colleges are expected to provide in return for public funds. The second is a systematic method of monitoring institutional performance.[4]

An exactly similar letter was sent to the Chairman of the UFC.

The letter also drew attention to the need for higher education institutions to earn income from other sources and the importance of the UFC and the PCFC encouraging them to do so.

The Act requires the Council to have regard to the desirability of not discouraging institutions from maintaining or developing their funding from other sources. I very much hope it will seek ways of actively encouraging institutions to increase their private earnings so that the State's share of institution's funding falls and the incentive to respond to the needs of students and employers is increased.[5]

On the question of fees the letter merely remarks that

various views have been put forward about the way in which the purchasing power of students might be given more prominence in the funding of higher education. While some of the possibilities which have been aired would take some time to implement, a more immediate possibility would be a shift in the current balance between the block grant and fees. I want to give further thought to this.[6]

Clearly fees and associated are still on the agenda but they are not part of the present instructions to the funding councils.

In brief, the central aim of present government policy remains as set out in the 1987 White Paper which preceded the Education Reform Act.[7] This is to make higher education institutions more accountable to their funding sources through the operation of market and quasi-market mechanisms. Although no legal penalties seem to be threatened if institutions are unable to meet their agreed commitments, their performance will undoubtedly be closely monitored and the councils will have the authority to reclaim funds that are not used in accordance with their wishes. Furthermore, performance on one round of contracts will undoubtedly influence the financial treatment received by an institution on subsequent occasions.

The reaction of the universities to these proposed changes has been almost universally suspicious, while the polytechnics and colleges have in general welcomed them. The explanation is that they started from different places. For the universities the shift has been from a broadly 'collegial' model of funding which allowed them to spend general grants in accordance with their own institutional priorities. The polytechnics, on the other hand, were subjected to a good deal of bureaucratic control from both their local authorities and central government. For the universities, therefore, exposure to the market represents a reduction in their institutional freedom, whereas for the polytechnics it represents an increase.

Apart from the vested interests of autonomous institutions, the main danger of market financing is that it will become progressively more difficult for higher education institutions to teach broadly cultural subjects or to teach other subjects in ways that do not promise an immediate economic return. It is also feared that basic fundamental research will be increasingly undervalued. These risks are exacerbated because the new arrangements are being implemented during a period of financial stringency and fears have been expressed that it will be difficult for universities and polytechnics to retain funds for fundamental research and teaching that is not geared to the needs of the labour market. The government has shown some recognition of these fears by announcing an intention to switch public funds from near-market research to more basic work.

However, the dominant influence on higher education finance during the 1990s will not be the Education Reform Act but the decline in the number of school leavers. Such a decrease has not occurred since the 1930s and there is no one in higher education who has practical experience of a situation in which the number of potential clients is decreasing from this dominant sector of the higher education market. Whether or not it will mean fewer actual students will depend on the responses of government and institutions. The government has made it clear that it expects to see big rises in participation rates with no increase in government funding. However, there must be many doubts about whether government will be able to resist pressures for financial incentives for students and institutions when manpower shortages, particularly in public sector activities such as teaching, begin really to bite in the early 1990s. For this reason alone it is fair to treat with a fair degree of scepticism the expectations that higher education in the 1990s will be simply a market-driven activity financed mainly out of student fees and employers' contributions.

There will be, of course, some members of the government who will see the fall in the number of traditional clients as an opportunity to reduce expenditure commitments still further. Their arguments will be strengthened by the fact that at the same time as the school-leaving population is falling the proportion of people above normal working age will be increasing rapidly. There will be a growing demand both for pension benefits and for medical and other services required by an ageing population. However, the attraction of reduced expenditure on higher education will be tempered by fears of shortages of highly-qualified entrants to the workforce. If the economy is to continue to grow at a healthy rate employers' demands for well-qualified workers will increase. Furthermore, as economic growth comes to depend more and more on high-technology goods and services, the standard of education of even the most highly-qualified workers will need to improve. The Council for Industry and Higher Education, in its influential policy statement in 1987, was already beginning to point out the dangers of an inadequate supply of highly-qualified entrants to the labour force.[8] In fact, demographic trends are likely to have their most damaging effects on public sector employment. In particular, demographic trends will lead to two more specific areas of qualified manpower shortage unless specific steps are take to counteract them: the first is in the area of medical care, especially care for elderly people; the second is school teaching, since the low numbers of births in the late 1960s and early 1970s have been replaced by larger birth cohorts reflecting the age structure of the population. In addition, there is good reason to believe that young people now reaching the age of entry to higher education are more likely to want to continue their studies than those from earlier generations. A much higher proportion of families now have at least one member who has experience of higher education and there is evidence that young persons from such families have a much higher than average propensity to enter higher education.

As far as governments are concerned, therefore, there will be two opposing pressures – to divert some public expenditure away from higher education towards those activities that cater for an ageing population, and conversely to meet the growing social demand and to increase both the teaching and research outputs of higher education so as to avoid bottlenecks to continued economic growth and social improvement. The desire for public expenditure restraint, accompanied by increased output of graduates, points to policies that will encourage efficiency, that will attract funding from sources other than government, that will be selective in their impact on different higher education activities, and that will maintain appropriate standards in increasingly diversified systems.

As far as the universities, polytechnics and colleges are concerned there will be increased competition among institutions and an emphasis on 'marketing' is inevitable. Universities will compete with each other for 'traditional' students and all institutions will try to increase participation from less traditional students. There will be growing emphasis on 'access' by students from disadvantaged backgrounds and ethnic minority groups and on the continuing education of adults. The growing tendency to see research as an activity separate from teaching is likely to be emphasized still further as research-intensive universities come to appreciate the advantages of separating them. There are obvious economies of concentration and scale if all research projects are required to make their appropriate contribution to overhead costs. In these circumstances a growing emphasis on quality assurance is inevitable.

The financial circumstances of UK higher education are clearly undergoing radical change. History will eventually decide whether the changes are inevitable and evolutionary, resulting from developments within the higher education system itself, or whether they are an aspect of a much wider shift in UK economic attitudes which occurred quite suddenly in 1980 or thereabouts. For anyone concerned with policy and management decisions in British universities, polytechnics and colleges such considerations are largely academic. The incontrovertible fact is that universities are now subject to a great deal more explicit accountability for the public funds they receive than was the case before 1980 and this accountability is likely to increase. For public sector institutions the bureaucratic accountability of line-by-line budgeting will diminish when they become independent statutory corporations. However, like the universities, their accountability to their funding agencies for the patterns and efficiency of their academic activities is likely to increase. All institutions are experiencing a considerable increase in the influence of market forces and they are now responding to the purchasing power of a wide variety of client, for example overseas students and their sponsors, the Training Agency, local authorities who have increased powers over teacher-training budgets, private industrial and commercial enterprises, government departments other than the DES (especially the Department of Trade and Industry), research councils and charitable foundations. These various 'customers' of higher education now account for very nearly half of the income of universities, compared with about a quarter in the early 1970s. It is a reasonable forecast that before the end of the century the figure will have risen to about two-thirds.

Students' fees, grants and loans

Financial aid to students is also undergoing major change. In the autumn of 1988 the government produced its long-awaited White Paper announcing its intention to introduce a loan scheme for those students entering higher education in the autumn of 1990.[9] The essence of the proposal is to peg undergraduate grants at their 1988–9 levels and for any increase in financial support to students to be in the form of loans made available through the banking system at a rate of interest equivalent to the rate of inflation. At current levels of inflation it is anticipated that by the year 2008 the costs of maintenance of the average undergraduate student will be shared as follows: government grant 29 per cent, bank loan 49 per cent, parents and students themselves 22 per cent. Despite signs of some resistance by the banks to the role carved out for them, it is probable that a loan scheme along these lines will come about. No major political party has committed itself to retaining the grant system in its present form and none has undertaken to abolish loans if they are introduced.

The wider debate about student finance is really concerned with two quite separate issues: whether a larger part of the income of higher education institutions should be in the form of fees paid by students; and whether financial support for student maintenance costs should be in the form of grants or loans.

The Robbins Committee believed that higher education institutions would be more independent and more efficient and responsive to the needs of society if they depended to a significant extent on the fees of students. Its report suggested that about 20 per cent of institutional income should be derived from fees.[10] This is not the same as recommending that students, or their families, should bear the costs. Individual students can be subsidized as easily as their institutions. At present home student fees account for about 5 per cent of university income and some 12 per cent of polytechnic income. However, most full-time students on undergraduate courses have this fee paid as part of their grant. This fact, that fees derive ultimately from public funds, led some observers, for example the 1986 Jarratt Committee,[11] to suggest that they should be abolished entirely. The Robbins Committee, however, took the more sophisticated view that 'it is a source of strength that public finance should come through more than one channel'.[12]

The Robbins recommendation was ignored. For a short period in the late 1970s home student fees were raised to a level where they accounted for nearly 25 per cent of the income of higher education institutions. This represented an income for some institutions that was higher than marginal costs, particularly on courses that were not recruiting well, and, therefore, there was an incentive for them to increase student numbers in order to obtain the fee income. After 1981 this was felt to be incompatible with the UGC strategy of maintaining the unit of resource and limiting student numbers. There was also concern in the Treasury, at a time of severe public expenditure restraint, that expenditure on students' fees could not easily be cash-limited. The government was, therefore, persuaded in 1981 to revert to a low-fees policy.

Although the introduction of a universal system of grants for fees and living expenses for all degree-level students was a major advance which facilitated the expansion of UK higher education in the 1960s and 1970s, other countries achieved even higher rates of growth with very different financial arrangements. There is now a widespread belief that the grants system no longer serves the best interests of the nation, or even of students themselves. It is thought to hinder, rather than encourage, the development of a larger, more open and more flexible system of higher education.

The most widely accepted criticism is that the declining real value of grants and the increasing severity of means-testing has resulted in a considerable proportion of students suffering financial hardship. Parental contributions now represent 37 per cent of the total maintenance costs of undergraduate students, compared with 20 per cent in 1979. Another widespread criticism is that the present grant system provides little incentive for universities or polytechnics to develop new types of courses to meet the changing needs of industry and the economy. There have been proposals for two-year pass degrees and more part-time undergraduate courses in universities, but the criteria for designation of courses which are eligible for mandatory grants discourage this kind of innovation. The government, along with many other commentators, now believes that instead of encouraging expansion as it did in the 1960s the present system of grants is a brake on expansion. There are some vice chancellors who see subsidies to students as being competitive with grants to institutions within a fixed total higher education budget.

Compared with most other countries of the Western world, the United Kingdom is unique in the extent to which it uses grants rather than loans as its principal form of financial support to undergraduate students, in the extent to which financial support is concentrated on a single type of course, and in the sharp distinction between full-time and part-time students in determining eligibility for support. But to attempt to provide mandatory grants at current levels for students who at present do not qualify would be prohibitively expensive and would condemn the country to an even more narrowly restrictive higher education system.

The view of the Robbins Committee was that since a degree gave most graduates considerably higher earnings than their less well-qualified contemporaries, there was no reason in principle why part of the financial support of the students should not be in the form of loans rather than grants. However, the Committee added that the low participation rate in UK higher education made it undesirable to introduce loans until 'the habit of higher education is more firmly established'.[13] Since that time there has been almost continuous debate inside and outside government about whether a student loans scheme should replace the present grant arrangements in whole or in part. The argument is largely about the likely effect on equity and economic efficiency.

In recent years, however, two new considerations have dominated the debate and converted many former opponents to favour at least a partial loans scheme. The proportion of national income devoted to student grants has increased by 150 per cent since 1961. It is now widely believed that this substantial commitment to student support is draining resources from more direct subsidy of higher education and associated activities. It is argued that a switch from grants to loans would not significantly discourage participation among young people from the social groups most likely to undertake higher education, and it would permit significant increases in the funds available for the institutions.

The second new theme in the debate is that the concentration of grants on full-time students doing first-degree courses has influenced the demand for higher education in a way and to an extent that is inequitable and economically inefficient. If the amount of public funds currently spent on student grants were redistributed more equitably, so that all students, full-time and part-time, were entitled to some grant, it would be necessary for full-time students, or their families, to contribute a larger share of their living expenses than they do at present. However, such a redistribution, supplemented by government-guaranteed loans to cover the difference between grants and living costs, would almost certainly increase the aggregate demand for higher education, though the pattern of that demand would be very different from the present one. There would be fewer full-time students on honours degree courses and more part-time students on other types of course. Proposals for such an extension were not included in the autumn 1988 White Paper.

Financial support for students can be advocated for two separate reasons. First, it may raise the total level of demand for higher education above what it would otherwise be. This may be justified at a time of labour shortages when high salaries and high levels of employment in the youth labour market might otherwise discourage young people from investing their time in obtaining higher-level qualifications. Second, financial support for students may be targeted so as to reduce inequalities between different social groups. Financial support is obviously more effective when the main reasons for non-participation are financial than when the reasons are cultural or social.

In the likely conditions of the labour market in the 1990s it is improbable that students' families will be required to pay substantially higher fees for conventional undergraduate courses. If it is decided that there are advantages in having a larger part of the income of institutions paid to them in the form of fees, a considerable proportion of these fee payments will need to be subsidized out of public funds in one form or another.

A more difficult issue is likely to be the finance of continuing education and postgraduate studies as these come to form a larger part of the activities of higher education institutions. It is in this area that employers will have a major part to play. Many though by no means all of the new courses will be vocationally orientated to meet specific employment needs in updating skills or providing retraining for those whose present range of skills has been made redundant by technological, economic or social change. Where the new skills offered are specific to the needs of particular employers or small groups of employers it is appropriate that they should meet most of the costs. In many cases, as at present, individual employers will continue to make specific arrangements with particular institutions. However public funds have a part to play in providing incentives especially for smaller employers, in ensuring that public sector agencies act as enlightened employers, releasing employees for continuing education, and in providing finance to help workers obtain new skills when those they have previously acquired have become redundant through technological or economic change.

The huge expansion of the Youth Training Scheme has introduced a new dimension to the student loans debate that has so far received little attention. It is in effect a subsidy scheme for young people who are not in higher education. In principle it is linked to training but it has the effect mainly of subsidizing the employment of young persons when they first enter the labour market. There is a danger that YTS generosity, combined with the emphasis on cost recovery in higher education, will lead to students, who used to be at an advantage as compared with their contemporaries in the amount of public money spent on them, being at a serious disadvantage, with serious long-term effects on the development of high-level skills. One obstacle to the resolution of such inconsistencies is that different government departments are involved with different priorities.

Serious consideration should be given to the possibility of developing co-ordinated schemes of income support for young persons during the period of transition between the completion of compulsory education and their establishment in the permanent labour force. The 1990s will be a period of youth shortage, with employers and higher education institutions competing for school leavers, so distortions in the incentive structure will have particularly damaging economic effects. The absence of serious overall youth unemployment will mean that the establishment of a comprehensive framework for youth support need not be prohibitively expensive.

The 1980s have not been an easy period for UK higher education. Many of its problems depended ultimately on fundamental demographic and economic forces. These were predictable and were predicted in the Report of the

Leverhulme Study at the beginning of the 1980s.[14] It is equally easy for a dispassionate observer to predict that the 1990s will see another swing of the pendulum. The most important feature is that graduate unemployment will recede into the past. There is some debate about whether humanities and social science graduates will ever again have such easy labour-market conditions as they did in the 1960s, but it is a fair bet that by the middle of the decade most graduates will again be choosing their employment rather than being chosen by employers. It is not at all impossible that well before the end of the century the complacent resistance to change of the late 1960s will have replaced the fawning anxiety to please which characterises much of the higher education debate today. In the final Leverhulme Volume we quoted Francis Bacon: 'Adversity is not without comforts and hopes. Prosperity doth best discover vice, but adversity doth best discover virtue . . .'[15] The adversity of the 1980s has brought out many virtues in our universities and polytechnics, including, despite all the adverse comment in the press and elsewhere, a remarkable ability, unequalled elsewhere in UK economic activity, to adapt to changing economic and political circumstances. It is to be hoped that these lessons remain well learned in a decade that promises to be one of great opportunity for most higher education institutions. At the end of the 1980s demand for higher education by school leavers is increasing against all expectations. There are huge increases in business funding of universities and polytechnics and these trends show every likelihood of increasing. The demand for a wide variety of continuing education is growing rapidly. None of these offer the security of the old UGC block grant or the Advanced Further Education Pool. But they do offer opportunities for well-managed, well-led and well-staffed universities, polytechnics and colleges.

Notes

1 Department of Education and Science *et al.*, *Top-up Loans for Students*, Cm 520, HMSO, 1988.
2 There will in fact be a slight difference in that most universities have a Royal Charter, whereas the polytechnics and colleges will be established as statutory corporations. For all practical purposes these are the same thing.
3 DES, *Higher Education: Meeting the Challenge*, Cm 114, HMSO, 1987.
4 Letters to the Chairmen of the UFC and the PCFC dated 31 October 1988.
5 Ibid.
6 Ibid.
7 DES, *Meeting the Challenge*.
8 Council for Industry and Higher Education, *Towards a Partnership: Higher Education-Government-Industry*, CIHE, 1987.
9 DES *et al.*, *Top-up Loans for Students*, Cm 520, HMSO, 1988.
10 Lord Chancellor's Office, *Higher Education*. Report of the Committee under the Chairmanship of Lord Robbins, HMSO, 1963.
11 Committee of Vice Chancellors and Principals, *Report of the Steering Group on University Efficiency*, CVCP, 1985.
12 Lord Chancellor's Office, *Higher Education*.

13 Ibid.
14 Leverhulme Report, *Excellence in Diversity*, SRHE, 1983.
15 G. Williams and T. Blackstone, *Response to Adversity*, SRHE, 1983.

Conclusion

Heather Eggins

New situations demand new strategies. The context of higher education today impresses upon us necessary new approaches. We live in a constantly shrinking world.

The technological revolution now brings into our homes satellite television; the time taken to move information from Australia to England has shrunk in a century from the many weeks of the sailing clipper to the split second of the satellite message. With speed has come cheapness: a faxed communication from Washington to London travels at a nominal cost. It ironically takes longer to deliver it by courier in London than to send it across the Atlantic. The explosion of the knowledge industry is intrinsically bound up with the growth of information technology.

With speed and ease of communication come our awareness of happenings in other places. World events impinge on our national consciousness in a manner that involves us, as watchers in our living room, more directly than before. The moment of the US Senate's decision to reject the President's nomination for Defence Secretary is brought before us. The agony of the starving children in the Sudan psychologically shakes us in a way that no ordered reporting, with its implication of distance and 'otherness', can do.

The global environment now directly affects our national consciousness. The day-by-day tale of the combined efforts of the Soviet Union and the United States to save the Arctic whales has an emotional grip on its viewers that betokens a growing sense of 'us' as part of and wholly involved in 'the world'. Concern about the rain forests of Brazil and the ozone layer over the Antarctic is genuine and widely shared. The United Kingdom is no longer 'us' and 'them': it is 'us' as part of the 'whole', no separated 'island'.

The implications for higher education follow: we are aware in an interested way of what is practised elsewhere in higher education. The Australian reforms are discussed avidly at London seminars; other models are assessed, ideas interchanged. Government has always kept itself informed of developments elsewhere: Matthew Arnold, as Inspector of Schools, regularly travelled the Continent to gather first-hand knowledge of other systems, but the open advocacy of the virtues of the US system by the UK Secretary of State for Education is new.

One can argue that this is part of the internationalization of higher education. Research has always been international: chemists have always read scientific German. Teaching has not been so. The recognition of the research world that knowledge must be made available throughout the globe is now shared by those concerned with the wider context of higher education. Conferences are international. Ideas offered in a single seminar can include those from Chinese, American, Turkish, and African contributors. The dominance of English as the supreme world language facilitates the exchanges.

Europe is particularly no longer 'other' and apart. Diana Green treats in detail the major effects of European harmonization on our higher education system. '1992' and the changes already in place will bring about a massive transition of thought and feeling which will reverberate throughout our system. The vision of up to 10 per cent of our students undertaking some study on the continent has profound repercussions. Likewise, the movement of continental students into the South-East of England will need to be provided for.

Another peculiar feature of our times is the demographic downturn. Curiously, the international situation during the 1990s and into the next century is one of huge and continuing Malthusian expansion. The sheer pressure of the world's burgeoning peoples on the space and resources of the globe will become one of the prevailing factors within next century's policies. At home the demographic trends move downwards for most of the next decade. The prospect of fewer new young graduates already causes anxiety to commerce and industry and is already, as Gareth Williams argues, having its effect on the financing and provision of higher education. There may possibly be another population bulge early in the next century but in the meantime severe difficulties could well be encountered by firms who wish to recruit, train and retain good-quality graduates.

The new era in which we live has to include a recognition of the resources available. We are not now a rich nation in terms of economic prosperity. The bonanza of North Sea oil is long since past. Now the emphasis is on conserving what wealth we have, anxious that oil reserves, despite new findings off the Dorset coast, may not last far into the next century. 'The most efficient use of what we have' is now the cry.

Money no longer flows for research. 'Well-found' laboratories still exist, but are fewer in number. No longer is the United Kingdom a leading research nation. Some commentators already speak of our being in the third division.

Higher education has as a whole been forced to prioritize. Resources have to be argued for, efficiency has to be proved. Some form of contract for the delivery of higher education appears inevitable. In the present climate the generally held view is that resources may shrink even more.

The new factors have brought in their wake a number of responses. To some extent these can be perceived as a stock-taking of where we are. In a nation of a declining labour force the recognition by government and society of people as assets is easy to support. The nineteenth-century argument for the individual worth of each person within society and, following from that, the need to structure society in such a way that each talent is maximized still has much to recommend it. The notion of the untapped pool of talented individuals capable of undertaking higher education surely underlies the Secretary of State's recent speeches. And there is sound evidence for this. Her Majesty's Inspectors in Newham found the normal range of IQs in the schools there, including the expected numbers of very bright children. Yet the local participation rate in higher education of 10.7 per cent for all higher education institutions and 3.4 per cent for universities in 1986–7 indicates that society is indeed failing to maximize the talents of its members.

Wastage can be condoned by some when labour is plentiful, but is unacceptable when industry and commerce are in danger of not functioning to full capacity because of shortages of trained personnel. The Council for Industry and Higher Education has made clear that the 1990s must produce more graduates capable of fulfilling the nation's requirements. The present system, unchanged, cannot deliver.

The new context has brought about a reassessment of objectives. Indeed, government has already put much effort into defining its objectives. The high profile given to work on higher education betokens a determination to think in terms of at least the next 25 years. Objectives agreed now, even if not fully adhered to, will have a major effect on the shape of future provision.

The reconsideration of what has been taken for granted in terms of the perception of higher education as primarily that of three-year full-time courses provided for 18-year-olds is now well under way. The question of the proper definition of higher education is raised in the Introduction and echoed by others in this volume. There is now a growing acceptance that a multitude of levels can quite properly be viewed as higher education: certificate, diploma and degree, postgraduate diploma, Masters and doctorate. The Open University has pioneered many imaginative approaches to the offering of modules and units at various levels. Huge modular structures of courses such as that at Oxford Polytechnic enable students to negotiate their learning and choose the level most suitable for their requirements. The definition of objectives directly affects the provision offered to the public.

Manpower planning has had a somewhat checkered history as an objective. Control over intakes is arguably the most direct way government has had of influencing the delivery of graduates. The teaching profession has long had precise numbers of places assigned to it. Such tight control of exact numbers in particular institutions has not always produced the end-product that was envisaged but one could say that there were good intentions. The National Advisory Body likewise imposed numbers but the new Polytechnics and Colleges Funding Council (PCFC) may well use a somewhat different formula.

The further objective of 'quality' is much discussed, with the Minister for Higher Education calling for a redefinition. The consensus appears to be a wish, even a yearning, to conserve and maintain the best of what we have traditionally offered, and simultaneously to develop ways of training the young adult minds so that they are enabled to contribute to society as fully participating individuals.

That carries with it Kenneth Wilson's recognition of the adult as one who can grapple with moral perspectives, as well as Geoffrey Harding's insistence that the model industrialist must by definition evince corporate social responsibility. The intention, as ever, is the development of the 'whole person', one who is able to gain knowledge for himself or herself, and able to take responsibility for his or her knowledge and skills: an intellectually prepared, properly functioning human being.

There are further objectives that commentators would like to see: the creation of higher education as a context which not only *includes* as many members of society as, in the White Paper's terms, have 'the necessary intellectual competence, motivation and maturity to benefit from higher education'[1] but also *involves* them in a multitude of roles. We are all students; at times we are all teachers; we are all, throughout our lives, inevitably caught up in life-long learning.

The notion of creating higher education institutions that are capable of liberating the energies of all members of that community, whether it be staff or students, still has much to commend it. The ability to foster innovative thinking and develop leadership potential in its members is still much valued. Our historical minds recognize that in the past Oxford and Cambridge colleges did provide exactly such an environment; the atmosphere of study and learning was contained; the system was closed. The image continues to be a powerful one, as Anthony O'Hear testifies.

The image worked for that world for a given period. But even then, Jude could not enter. The closed community, though appealing, is maintained at too great a cost for the society in which we now find ourselves – many, many more people; much more demand for access; much faster and more widespread access to knowledge. Indeed, if knowledge is seen as power, then the continuance of an elite system carries with it implications of oligarchy that are not now acceptable within society.

A major response to the new context has been a concern with access. Indeed, the drive to expand access to higher education has become urgent. Governments are stimulated by demography. Demand has already risen from an age participation index of 12 per cent in 1979 to one of 14.2 per cent in 1986. The recent White Paper allows a target of 18.5 per cent, the Secretary of State talks of 30 per cent.[2] The intellectual arguments for expanding continuing education and for opening access have been thoroughly rehearsed a number of years ago,[3] but the will to expand access has only recently been discovered. Even now there are some hesitations, as evinced in Anthony O'Hear's paper and alluded to in Victoria Phillips's paper, for fear that more might just mean worse.

The key to access will lie with the attitudes of institutions. The numbers of 18-year-olds entering the system will not show any dramatic rise, particularly if A levels are not reformed and if there is no financial provision for 16–18-year-olds. The prospect of money at 16 for those whose families cannot afford to maintain students through the sixth-form years, might make a difference, however. Cogent arguments for educational entitlements at 16 were put as long ago as 1978,[4] in the Birley Report and there are now a growing number of voices who point out that the multitude of Youth Training Schemes offered to that age range could well be having a deleterious effect on the number who choose to continue academic studies.

The mature age groups of those in their twenties and thirties, as Leslie Wagner indicates, may well produce many more potential recruits than at present. As time moves into the next century the healthy and powerful group of senior citizens are very likely to clamour for access. The University of the Third Age is already established in one or two places, notably at Lancaster University. Their ability to pay as well as their interest and motivation will have its effect on the system.

New situations produce new academic strategies. Those institutions who determine to respond to the new situation will survive: those who choose not to do so will run the risk of becoming marginalized. There is always a place in a system for the purveyor of specialized high-class goods but the small scale of such operations makes the 'little men' a prey to merger mania.

Changes in the management structures of institutions have arguably developed in response to new developments. The traditional university pattern of a Senate which lumbered to decisions on new courses, and frequently saw fit not to approve innovative suggestions has given way to Jarratt-like management structures, with the vice chancellor as chief executive, leading a team of professionally trained officers. The decision-making structures are clearly defined and set up in such a way that new developments, if sound, can be encouraged. The ability to respond to change is now seen as a 'given' of institutional management.

Finance, too, has been responsive to change. Gareth Williams traces the prospects for the funding of higher education in his paper. Suffice it to say that more students have to be brought into the system. The present funding arrangements could not support them: the future pattern, in detail, still awaits determination.

Institutional responses to the new context are already producing new shapes, new curricular designs, more flexible modes of learning, new approaches, such as credit accumulation and transfer, and a new interpretation of locale. Curriculum change has been partially fostered by pressure from employers. Peter Slee argues that the transition to the world of work for the young graduate can best be managed by providing him or her with a series of core skills. Capability can be achieved, in his thinking, without undermining the academic disciplines. The Training Agency, with its Enterprise in Higher Education initiative, has had a marked effect in encouraging academics to re-examine their curricula in terms of enterprise. The Royal Society of Arts' notion of 'capability' in higher education is attracting serious attention. Deliberate, well-considered changes are being made: the opportunity for humanities students to develop numeracy and information technology skills is now more readily available, the opportunity for engineers to make cogent, well-argued presentations comes more often. Work placement and work shadowing are deemed to have a usefulness for the student that would have scarcely been considered a few years ago. But UK academics think carefully before embarking on curriculum change. The call for 'relevance' is unlikely to be allowed to weaken the rigour of academic disciplines.

The student as customer brings his or her own pressure to bear on the curriculum. He or she is likely to demand convenience, high quality of presentation, and usefulness as well as value for money. The assessment of teaching is in itself a response to change. The student's pattern of demand might vary at different periods of his or her life between career-orientated courses, and courses for his or her own individual satisfaction – learning, one might say, for the sake of learning. Considered in this light the study of philosophy is just as 'useful' as that of patent law. Both serve the particular purpose of the particular student at a particular time.

Modes of learning offer new shapes for higher education. A mix of full-time and part-time study is much more accepted now. Courses pursued by distance learning will become much more common. Telephone and video conferencing, combined with all the panoply developed by the Open University, will be available as support. Interactive software and online data can enable the students to study at their own pace in their own time. Peer assessment and peer tutoring are natural developments for those who believe that mature students can be responsible for their own learning. The fixed pattern of attendance at lectures, full-time, in a particular place, has many alternatives.

Perhaps the most revolutionary new 'shape' is that of the introduction of the system of credit accumulation and transfer. The approach to higher education as affording a series of building blocks, which are interchangeable between institutions, owes much to the US system of credit transfer arrangements. The British system, pioneered by the agreement between the Council for National Academic Awards (CNAA) and the Open University, is expanding steadily, not only among UK institutions across the sectors but also into Europe, and into industry and commerce. The possibilities of the system offer a flexible tool superbly fitted to fulfil the needs of the mature student in a dynamic environment and to offer a route for the recognition of work-based learning. When the development of ways of recognizing experiential learning are added to this, one has a means of not only recognizing learning related to paid employment but also the possibility of accommodating as valuable within society the skills developed in a woman's child-bearing years, her life experience of rearing children and of organizing a household.

The most all-encompassing new dimension for higher education in the 1990s and beyond is the reinterpretation of the term 'institution'. The notion of travelling to a specific place of higher education began to wither with the founding of the Open University and now is likely to become less and less the norm. The most apt image for higher education is no longer an 'ivory tower'. Perhaps a 'blood circulatory system' would be suitable, with higher education informing the whole of society, providing it with energy and maintaining its overall health. This might appear to be a heady image which is easy to dispute if one retreats to a separatist tradition, but even if one accepts that higher education evinces 'a dynamic conservatism traditionally charged with conserving and transmitting rather than with innovating'[5] the metaphor points to the possibility of new forms taking shape.

New clients for higher education, as Gareth Williams points out, abound. They include overseas students, local authorities, private and commercial enterprises, government departments such as the Department of Trade and Industry, and the Training Agency. The financial partnerships thus engendered encourage the development of flexible and varied structures of management and methods of delivery. International and European links are being constantly strengthened. Innovatory teaching schemes can include the offering of part of a degree course abroad followed by the final part resident at the university in the United Kingdom. The client or customer has to some extent the power to dictate his or her terms. UK higher education can be packaged and marketed abroad, its staff can teach abroad. The Open University, as ever the pioneer, offers its courses in Ireland and Belgium, as well as its expertise in establishing open universities in countries such as Pakistan. The convention that one travels to an institution in the United Kingdom in order to obtain higher education is swept aside under the pressure of Europe, of international demands and by the technological revolution.

The requirements of industry are similarly leading to the development of new patterns of provision. The CNAA already has in place procedures for the validation and review of courses offered by employers. These are normally designed in collaboration with one or more higher education institutions and are offered jointly. The case study of IBM in this volume indicates how their scheme works. Interestingly, though, the CNAA also allows employers to propose courses independently of any institution of higher education. Clearly such arrangements are most likely to be found most frequently in large companies which possess a training centre, but the fact that such an arrangement is sought by employers, and can be accommodated, indicates how the UK system of higher education can respond to the new context in which it finds itself. This, too, has fascinating repercussions in that it would be feasible for a major international company to offer a validated course throughout its network with the possibility that the whole of a UK validated course might be pursued outside the geographical location of the United Kingdom. It is not without significance that one of the principal changes in the CNAA charter was the addition of an international dimension. Higher education as export is already being given serious consideration by entrepreneurial institutions.

The anticipated demographic changes, it could be argued, have directly aided the development of courses offered by employers. As the 18-year-old cohort declines, the competition for the best becomes fiercer. Clearly the employer who can offer bright 18-year-olds both a salary *and* a degree simultaneously, particularly a degree whose curriculum is as up-to-date and relevant as the employer can make it, must be in a strong position to get the employees required. The result for both employee, employer and any associated institution must have much to recommend it.

Companies offering tailor-made courses have other advantages. They may well need to train not only their own workforce in particular areas, but also those of their suppliers. The validation of a purpose-built package, which in itself is allotted points within the credit accumulation and transfer scheme, enables the networking of training to take place throughout the employer's system. The 'circulation of the blood' image holds true.

The pattern of applications for credit rating is in itself an indicator of the growing flexibility of higher education provision. The somewhat artificial division in the past between higher education and training is gradually breaking down. The range of bodies making enquiries includes not only companies but also training centres and professional bodies. The list is constantly expanding.

The recognition of experiential learning furthers the process, so much so that the award of postgraduate qualifications based on a mix of professional study and professional experience pursued within a company becomes possible. If one turns back to the Secretary of State's figure of 30 per cent participation rate in higher education and thinks of this not just in terms of the institutions as we now know them, but in terms of the immense possibilities for permeating industry and commerce with higher education, then it appears somewhat less of a pipe-dream. The procedures are already in place to a great extent: the motivation of industry to find and to retain the highest quality of employee that it can, in view of the demographic context, is almost guaranteed to bring about a massive expansion on these lines. The imaginative, innovative institution will respond positively; the traditional one will maintain an ostrich-like position until it is too late.

Locale is affected by the view of student as customer and the whole community as groups to be wooed with the offerings of higher education. The good salesman takes his custom into the place where his potential customers are. The Committee of Enquiry into Higher Education for Newham argues for targeting higher education to different groups in different ways, for the expansion of access courses, for the opening up of higher education facilities, for the use of a wide range of places where people are – local firms, schools, community centres.[6] It is psychologically much easier for a mother with small children living in a close-knit Indian or Pakistan community to pursue a first year in higher education when she can study in a small group round the corner with other neighbours. The projected London Docklands consortium plans to take exactly this marketing approach, actively recruiting young people and adults in the region, guaranteeing access to higher education to those demonstrating their likelihood of deriving benefit, and working, as appropriate, across institutional barriers.

Finally, though, there has to be a recognition that there is more than one road open. Students, staff, institutions and government are faced with choices that can lead either to Peter Scott's 'shrunken horizons' or to innovation and expansion. The warnings of *Future Shock*[7] still stand.

This book, then, does not claim to define the future of higher education with any exactitude. We are not crystal-ball gazers. What it does claim, though, is to offer an examination of the trends of thinking and a consideration of new developments. Analysis of where we are and where we appear to be going sharpens our abilities to assess our aims and adjust our planning for the 1990s and beyond. 'The road not taken' can at least be indicated; the choices are still to be made. We offer this book to the reader in the hope that it might enable him or her to escape somewhat from being trapped within the constraints of now, and be aided in reaching decisions as to the shape of higher education that will best serve us all as clients, consumers and providers into the twenty-first century.

Notes

1 *Higher Education: Meeting the Challenge*, HMSO, Cm 114, April 1987, p. 7.
2 Ibid. p. 6; 'Baker's Vision for the Next 25 Years', *Times Higher Education Supplement*, 13 January 1989, p. 7.
3 ACACE, *Continuing Education: From Policies to Practice*, 1982.
4 *Opportunities at Sixteen: Report of a Study Group*, chaired by Derek Birley, HMSO Belfast, October 1978.
5 Chris Duke, 'The Future Shape of Continuing Education and Universities: an Inaugural Lecture' *Papers in Continuing Education*, No. 1, p. 18, University of Warwick, 1988.
6 Report of the Committee of Enquiry into Higher Education for Newham (The Toyne Enquiry), London Borough of Newham, July 1989.
7 Alvin Toffler, *Future Shock*, Bodley Head, 1970.

Index

The Society for Research into Higher Education

The Society exists both to encourage and co-ordinate research and development into all aspects of higher education, including academic, organizational and policy issues; and also to provide a forum for debate – verbal and printed.

The Society's income derives from subscriptions, book sales, conference fees, and grants. It receives no subsidies and is wholly independent. Its corporate members are institutions of higher education, research institutions and professional, industrial, and governmental bodies. Its individual members include teachers and researchers, administrators and students. Members are found in all parts of the world and the Society regards its international work as amongst its most important activities.

The Society discusses and comments on policy, organizes conferences, and encourages research. Under the imprint SRHE & OPEN UNIVERSITY PRESS, it is a specialist publisher of research, having some 40 titles in print. It also publishes *Studies in Higher Education* (three times a year) which is mainly concerned with academic issues; *Higher Education Quarterly* (formerly *Universities Quarterly*) mainly concerned with policy issues; *Abstracts* (three times a year); an *International Newsletter* (twice a year) and *SRHE NEWS* (four times a year).

The Society's committees, study groups and branches are run by members (with help from a small secretariat at Guildford), and aim to provide a forum for discussion. The groups at present include a Teacher Education Study Group, a Staff Development Group, and a Continuing Education Group, each of which may have their own organization, subscriptions, or publications (e.g. the *Staff Development Newsletter*). A further *Questions of Quality* Group has organized a series of Anglo-American seminars in the USA and the UK.

The Governing Council, elected by members, comments on current issues; and discusses policies with leading figures, notably at its evening forums. The Society organizes seminars on current research, and is in touch with bodies in the UK such as the PCFC, CVCP, UFC, CNAA and with sister-bodies overseas. It co-operates with the British Council on courses run in conjunction with its conferences.

The Society's conferences are often held jointly; and have considered '*Standards and Criteria*' (1986, with Bulmershe College); '*Restructuring*' (1987, with the City of Birmingham Polytechnic); '*Academic Freedom*' (1988, with the University of Surrey). In 1989, '*Access and Institutional Change*' (with the Polytechnic of North London). In 1990, the topic will be '*Industry and Higher Education*' (with the University of Surrey). In 1991, the topic will be '*Research in HE*'. Other conferences have considered the DES '*Green Paper*' (1985); '*HE After the Election*' (1987) and '*After the Reform Act*' (July 1988). An annual series on '*The First Year Experience*' with the University of South Carolina and Teesside Polytechnic held two meetings in 1988 in Cambridge, and another in St Andrew's in July 1989.

For some of the Society's conferences, special studies are commissioned in advance, as *Precedings*.

Members receive free of charge the Society's *Abstracts*, annual conference proceedings, (or 'Precedings'), *SRHE News* and *International Newsletter*. They may buy *SRHE & Open University Press* books at discount, and *Higher Education Quarterly* on special terms. Corporate members also receive the Society's journal *Studies in Higher Education* free (individuals on special terms). Members may also obtain certain other journals at a discount, including the NFER *Register of Educational Research*. There is a substantial discount to members, and to staff of corporate members, on annual and some other conference fees.

Further information: SRHE at the University, Guildford. GU2 5XH UK (0483) 39003